Language education

Frances Christie

Series Editor: Frances Christie

Oxford University Press
1989

Oxford University Press
Walton Street, Oxford OX2 6DP

Oxford   New York   Toronto
Delhi   Bombay   Calcutta   Madras   Karachi
Petaling Jaya   Singapore   Hong Kong   Tokyo
Nairobi   Dar es Salaam   Cape Town
Melbourne   Auckland

and associated companies in
Berlin   Ibadan

Oxford English and the *Oxford English* logo are trade marks of
Oxford University Press

ISBN 019 437152 2

Printed in Hong Kong.

About the author

Frances Christie

Frances Christie is a Senior Lecturer in Education and chairperson of the course *Language and Learning*, and also of its sequel, *Sociocultural Aspects of Language and Education*. She began her professional career as a teacher of English and history in secondary schools in New South Wales, though she also taught in London in the 1960s. She subsequently moved into teacher education and also worked for four years at the Curriculum Development Centre in Canberra, where she was responsible for the national Language Development Project. She has a particular interest in the study of the role of language in education.

Foreword

In a sense, educational interest in language is not new. Studies of rhetoric and of grammar go back as far as the Greeks; in the English-speaking countries, studies of the classical languages, and more recently of English itself, have had a well established place in educational practice. Moreover, a number of the issues which have aroused the most passionate debates about how to develop language abilities have tended to remain, resurfacing at various points in history in somewhat different formulations perhaps, but nonetheless still there, and still lively.

Of these issues, probably the most lively has been that concerning the extent to which explicit knowledge about language on the part of the learner is a desirable or a useful thing. But the manner in which discussion about this issue has been conducted has often been allowed to obscure other and bigger questions: questions, for example, both about the nature of language as an aspect of human experience, and about language as a resource of fundamental importance in the building of human experience. The tendency in much of the western intellectual tradition has been to dissociate language and experience, in such a way that language is seen as rather neutral, merely serving to 'carry' the fruits of experience. Whereas in this view language is seen as a kind of 'conduit', subservient to experience in various ways, an alternative view, as propounded in the books in this series, would argue that language is itself not only a part of experience, but intimately involved in the manner in which we construct and organise experience. As such, it is never neutral, but deeply implicated in building meaning. One's notions concerning how to teach about language will differ quite markedly, depending upon the view one adopts concerning language and experience. In fact, though discussions concerning teaching about language can sometimes be interesting, in practice many such discussions have proved theoretically ill-founded and barren, serving merely to perpetuate a number of unhelpful myths about language.

The most serious and confusing of these myths are those which would suggest we can dissociate language from meaning — form from function, or form from 'content'. Where such myths apply, teaching about language becomes a matter of teaching about 'language rules' — normally grammatical rules — and as history has demonstrated over the years, such teaching rapidly degenerates into the arid pursuit of parts of speech and the parsing of isolated sentences. Meaning, and the critical role of language in the building of meaning, are simply overlooked, and the kinds of knowledge about language made available to the learner are of a very limited kind.

The volumes in this series of monographs devoted to language education in my view provide a much better basis upon which to address questions related to the teaching about language than has been the case anywhere in the English-speaking world for some time now. I make this claim for several reasons, one of the most important being that the series never sought directly to establish a model for teaching about language at all. On the contrary, it sought to establish a principled model of language, which, once properly articulated, allows us to address many questions of an educational nature, including those to do with teaching about language. To use Halliday's term (1978), such a model sees language primarily as a 'social semiotic', and as a resource for meaning, centrally involved in the processes by which human beings negotiate, construct and change the nature of social experience. While the series certainly does not claim to have had the last word on these and related subjects, I believe it does do much to set a new educational agenda — one which enables us to look closely at the role of language both in living and in learning: one which, moreover, provides a basis upon which to decide those kinds of teaching and learning about language which may make a legitimate contribution to the development of the learner.

I have said that arguments to do with teaching about language have been around for a long time: certainly as long as the two hundred years of white settlement in Australia. In fact, coincidentally, just as the first settlers were taking up their enforced residence in the Australian colony of New South Wales, Lindley Murray was preparing his *English Grammar* (1795), which, though not the only volume produced on the subject in the eighteenth century, was certainly the best. Hundreds of school grammars that were to appear in Britain and Australia for the next century at least, were to draw very heavily upon what Murray had written. The parts of speech, parsing and sentence analysis, the latter as propounded by Morell (an influential inspector of schools in England), were the principal elements in the teaching about language in the Australian colonies, much as they were in England throughout the century. By the 1860s and 1870s the Professor of Classics and Logic at Sydney University, Charles Badham, who had arrived from England in 1867, publicly disagreed with the examining authorities in New South Wales concerning the teaching of grammar. To the contemporary reader there is a surprising modernity about many of his objections, most notably his strongly held conviction that successful control of one's language is learned less as a matter of committing to memory the parts of speech and the principles of parsing, than as a matter of frequent opportunity for use.

Historically, the study by which issues of use had been most effectively addressed had been that of rhetoric, in itself quite old in the English-speaking tradition, dating back at least to the sixteenth century. Rhetorical studies flourished in the eighteenth century, the best known works on the subject being George Campbell's *The Philosophy of Rhetoric* (1776), and Hugh Blair's *Lectures on Rhetoric and Belles Lettres* (1783), while in the nineteenth century Richard Whately published his work, *Elements of Rhetoric* (1828). As the nineteenth century proceeded, scholarly work on rhetoric declined, as was testified by the markedly

vi

inferior but nonetheless influential works of Alexander Bain (*English Composition and Rhetoric*, 1866; Revised version, 1887). Bain, in fact, did much to corrupt and destroy the older rhetorical traditions, primarily because he lost sight of the need for a basic concern with meaning in language. Bain's was the century of romanticism after all: on the one hand, Matthew Arnold was extolling the civilising influence of English literature in the development of children; on the other hand, there was a tendency towards suspicion, even contempt, for those who wanted to take a scholarly look at the linguistic organisation of texts, and at the ways in which they were structured for the building of meaning. In 1921, Ballard (who was an expert witness before the Newbolt Enquiry on the teaching of English), wrote a book called *Teaching the Mother Tongue*, in which he noted among other things, that unfortunately in England at least rhetorical studies had become associated with what were thought to be rather shallow devices for persuasion and argument. The disinclination to take seriously the study of the rhetorical organisation of texts gave rise to a surprisingly unhelpful tradition for the teaching of literature, which is with us yet in many places: 'civilising' it might be, but it was *not* to be the object of systematic study, for such study would in some ill-defined way threaten or devalue the work of literature itself.

A grammarian like Murray had never been in doubt about the relationship of grammar and rhetoric. As he examined it, grammar was concerned with the syntax of the written English sentence: it was not concerned with the study of 'style', about which he wrote a short appendix in his original grammar, where his debt to the major rhetoricians of the period was apparent. Rhetorical studies, especially as discussed by Campbell for instance, did address questions of 'style', always from the standpoint of a recognition of the close relationship of language to the socially created purpose in using language. In fact, the general model of language as discussed by Campbell bore some relationship to the model taken up in this series, most notably in its commitment to register.

The notion of register proposes a very intimate relationship of text to context: indeed, so intimate is that relationship, it is asserted, that the one can only be interpreted by reference to the other. Meaning is realised in language (in the form of text), which is thus shaped or patterned in response to the context of situation in which it is used. To study language then, is to concentrate upon exploring how it is systematically patterned towards important social ends. The linguistic theory adopted here is that of systemic linguistics. Such a linguistic theory is itself also a social theory, for it proposes firstly, that it is in the nature of human behaviour to build reality and/or experience through complex semiotic processes, and secondly, that the principal semiotic system available to humans is their language. In this sense, to study language is to explore some of the most important and pervasive of the processes by which human beings build their world.

I originally developed the volumes in this series as the basis of two major off campus courses in Language Education taught in the Master's degree program at Deakin University, Victoria, Australia. To the best of my knowledge, such courses, which are designed primarily for teachers and teacher educators, are the first of their kind in the world, and while they actually appeared in the mid 1980s, they emerge from work in language education which has been going on in Australia for some time. This included the national Language Development Project, to which Michael Halliday was consultant, and whose work I co-ordinated throughout its second, productive phase. (This major project was initiated by the Commonwealth Government's Curriculum Development Centre, Canberra, in the 1970s, and involved the co-operation of curriculum development teams from all Australian states in developing language curriculum materials. Its work was not completed because of political changes which caused the activities of the Curriculum Development Centre to be wound down.) In the 1980s a number of conferences have been held fairly regularly in different parts of Australia, all of them variously exploring aspects of language education, and leading to the publication of a number of conference reports. They include: Frances Christie (ed.), *Language and the Social Construction of Experience* (Deakin University, 1983); Brendan Bartlett and John Carr (eds.), *Language in Education Workshop: a Report of Proceedings* (Centre for Research and Learning, Brisbane C.A.E., Mount Gravatt Campus, Brisbane, 1984); Ruqaiya Hasan (ed.), *Discourse on Discourse* (Applied Linguistics Association of Australia, Occasional Papers, Number 7, 1985); Clare Painter and J.R. Martin (eds.), *Writing to Mean: Teaching Genres across the Curriculum* (Applied Linguistics Association of Australia, Occasional Papers, Number 9, 1986); Linda Gerot, Jane Oldenburg and Theo Van Leeuwen (eds.), *Language and Socialisation: Home and School* (in preparation). All these activities have contributed to the building of a climate of opinion and a tradition of thinking about language which made possible the development of the volumes in this series.

While it is true that the developing tradition of language education which these volumes represent does, as I have noted, take up some of the concerns of the older rhetorical studies, it nonetheless also looks forward, pointing to ways of examining language which were not available in earlier times. For example, the notion of language as a social semiotic, and its associated conception of experience or reality as socially built and constantly subject to processes of transformation, finds very much better expression today than would have been possible before, though obviously much more requires to be said about this than can be dealt with in these volumes. In addition, a functionally driven view of language is now available, currently most completely articulated in Halliday's *An Introduction to Functional Grammar* (1985), which offers ways of understanding the English language in a manner that Murray's Grammar could not have done.

Murray's Grammar confined itself to considerations of the syntax of the written English sentence. It did not have anything of use to say about spoken language, as opposed to written language, and, equally, it provided no basis upon which to explore a unit other than the sentence, whether that be the paragraph, or, even more importantly, the total text. The preoccupation with the written sentence reflected the pre-eminent position being accorded to the written word by Murray's time, leading to disastrous consequences since, that is the diminished value accorded to spoken language, especially in educational practices. In Murray's work, the lack of a direct relationship between the study of grammar on the one hand, and that of 'style', on the other hand, was, as I have already noted, to be attributed to his view that it was the rhetorician who addressed wider questions relating to the text. In the tradition in which he worked, in fact, grammar looked at syntactic rules divorced from considerations of meaning or social purpose.

By contrast, Halliday's approach to grammar has a number of real strengths, the first of which is the fact that its basis is semantic, not syntactic: that is to say, it is a semantically driven grammar, which, while not denying that certain principles of syntax do apply, seeks to consider and identify the role of various linguistic items in any text in terms of their function in building meaning. It is for this reason that its practices for interpreting and labelling various linguistic items and groupings are functionally based, not syntactically based. There is in other words, no dissociation of 'grammar' on the one hand and 'semantics' or meaning on the other. A second strength of Halliday's approach is that it is not uniquely interested in written language, being instead committed to the study of both the spoken and written modes, and to an explanation of the differences between the two, in such a way that each is illuminated because of its contrast with the other. A third and final strength of the systemic functional grammar is that it permits useful movement across the text, addressing the manner in which linguistic patternings are built up for the construction of the overall text in its particular 'genre', shaped as it is in response to the context of situation which gave rise to it.

Halliday's functional grammar lies behind all ten volumes in this series, though one other volume, by Michael Christie, called *Aboriginal perspectives on experience and learning: the role of language in Aboriginal Education*, draws upon somewhat different if still compatible perspectives in educational and language theory to develop its arguments. The latter volume, is available directly from Deakin University. In varying ways, the volumes in this series provide a helpful introduction to much that is more fully dealt with in Halliday's Grammar, and I commend the series to the reader who wants to develop some sense of the ways such a body of linguistic theory can be applied to educational questions. A version of the grammar specifically designed for teacher education remains to be written, and while I cherish ambitions to begin work on such a version soon, I am aware that others have similar ambitions — in itself a most desirable development.

While I have just suggested that the reader who picks up any of the volumes in this series should find ways to apply systemic linguistic theory to educational theory, I want to argue, however, that what is offered here is more than merely a course in applied linguistics, legitimate though such a course might be. Rather, I want to claim that this is a course in educational linguistics, a term of importance because it places linguistic study firmly at the heart of educational enquiry. While it is true that a great deal of linguistic research of the past, where it did not interpret language in terms of interactive, social processes, or where it was not grounded in a concern for meaning, has had little of relevance to offer education, socially relevant traditions of linguistics like that from which systemics is derived, do have a lot to contribute. How that contribution should be articulated is quite properly a matter of development in partnership between educationists, teachers and linguistics, and a great deal has yet to be done to achieve such articulation.

I believe that work in Australia currently is making a major contribution to the development of a vigorous educational linguistics, not all of it of course in a systemic framework. I would note here the important work of such people as J.R. Martin, Joan Rothery, Suzanne Eggins and Peter Wignell of the University of Sydney, investigating children's writing development; the innovatory work of Brian Gray and his colleagues a few years ago in developing language programs for Aboriginal children in central Australia, and more recently his work with other groups in Canberra; the recent work of Beth Graham, Michael Christie and Stephen Harris, all of the Northern Territory Department of Education, in developing language programs for Aboriginal children; the important work of John Carr and his colleagues of the Queensland Department of Education in developing new perspectives upon language in the various language curriculum guidelines they have prepared for their state; the contributions of Jenny Hammond of the University of Wollongong, New South Wales, in her research into language development in schools, as well as the various programs in which she teaches; research being undertaken by Ruqaiya Hasan and Carmel Cloran of Macquarie University, Sydney, into children's language learning styles in the transition years from home to school; investigations by Linda Gerot, also of Macquarie University, into classroom discourse in the secondary school, across a number of different subjects; and the work of Pam Gilbert of James Cook University, Townsville, in Queensland, whose interests are both in writing in the secondary school, and in language and gender.

The signs are that a coherent educational linguistics is beginning to appear around the world, and I note with pleasure the appearance of two new and valuable international journals: *Language and Education*, edited by David Corson of Massey University, New Zealand, and *Linguistics in Education*, edited by David Bloome, of the University of Massachusetts. Both are committed to the development of an educational linguistics, to which many traditions of study, linguistic, semiotic and sociological, will no doubt make an important contribution. Such an educational linguistics is long overdue, and in what are politically difficult times, I suggest such a study can make a major contribution to the pursuit of educational equality of opportunity, and to attacking the wider social problems of equity and justice. Language is a political institution: those who are wise in its ways, capable of using it to shape and serve important personal and social goals, will be the ones who are 'empowered' (to use a fashionable word): able, that is, not merely to participate effectively *in* the world, but able also *to act upon it*, in the sense that they can strive for significant social change. Looked at in these terms, provision of appropriate language education programs is a profoundly important matter, both in ensuring equality of educational opportunity, and in helping to develop those who are able and willing to take an effective role in democratic processes of all kinds.

One of the most encouraging measures of the potential value of the perspectives open to teachers taking up an educational linguistics of the kind offered in these monographs, has been the variety of teachers attracted to the courses of which they form a part, and the ways in which these teachers have used what they have learned in undertaking research papers for the award of the master's degree. They include, for example, secondary teachers of physics, social science, geography and English, specialists in teaching English as a second language to migrants and specialists in teaching English to Aboriginal people, primary school teachers, a nurse educator, teachers of illiterate adults, and language curriculum consultants, as well as a number of teacher educators with specialist responsibilities in teaching language education. For many of these people the perspectives offered by an educational linguistics are both new and challenging, causing them to review and change aspects of their teaching practices in various ways. Coming to terms with a semantically driven grammar is in itself quite demanding, while there is often considerable effort involved to bring to conscious awareness the ways in which we use language for the realisation of different meanings. But the effort is plainly worth it, principally because of the added sense of control and direction it can give teachers interested to work at fostering and developing students who are independent and confident in using language for the achievement of various goals. Those people for whom these books have proved helpful, tend to say that they have achieved a stronger and richer appreciation of language and how it works than they had before; that because they know considerably more about language themselves, they are able to intervene much more effectively in directing and guiding those whom they teach; that because they have a better sense of the relationship of language and 'content' than they had before, they can better guide their students into control of the 'content' of the various subjects for which they are responsible; and finally, that because they have an improved sense of how to direct language learning, they are able to institute new assessment policies, negotiating, defining and clarifying realistic goals for their students. By any standards, these are considerable achievements.

As I draw this Foreword to a close, I should perhaps note for the reader's benefit the manner in which students doing course work with me are asked to read the monographs in this series, though I should stress that the books were deliberately designed to be picked up and read in any order one likes. In the first of the two semester courses, called *Language and Learning*, students are asked to read the following volumes in the order given:

Frances Christie — *Language education*
Clare Painter — *Learning the mother tongue*
M.A.K. Halliday & Ruqaiya Hasan — *Language, context, and
    text: aspects of language in a social-semiotic perspective*
J.L. Lemke — *Using language in the classroom*
then either,
M.A.K. Halliday — *Spoken and written language*
or,
Ruqaiya Hasan — *Linguistics, language, and verbal art.*

The following four volumes, together with the one by Michael Christie, mentioned above, belong to the second course called *Sociocultural Aspects of Language and Education*, and they may be read by the students in any order they like, though only three of the five need be selected for close study:

David Butt — *Talking and thinking: the patterns of
    behaviour*
Gunther Kress — *Linguistic processes in sociocultural practice*
J.R. Martin — *Factual writing: exploring and challenging
    social reality*
Cate Poynton — *Language and gender: making the difference*

References

Bain, A., *An English Grammar* (Longman, Roberts and Green, London, 1863).

Bain, A., *English Composition and Rhetoric*, revised in two Parts — *Part 1, Intellectual Elements of Style*, and *Part 11, Emotional Qualities of Style* (Longman, Green and Company, London, 1887).

Ballard, P., *Teaching the Mother Tongue* (Hodder & Stoughton, London, 1921).

Blair, H., *Lectures on Rhetoric and Belles Lettres, Vols. 1 and 11* (W. Strahan and T. Cadell, London, 1783).

Campbell, G., (new ed.), *The Philosophy of Rhetoric* (T. Tegg and Son, London, 1838). Originally published (1776).

Halliday, M.A.K., *Language as social semiotic: the social interpretation of language and meaning* (Edward Arnold, London, 1978).

Halliday, M.A.K., *An Introduction to Functional Grammar* (Edward Arnold, London, 1985).

Murray, Lindley, *English Grammar* (1795), Facsimile Reprint No. 106 (Menston, Scolar Press, 1968).

Contents

Chapter 1

Language as a resource with which to structure and organise experience and meaning

If we were to conduct a survey of community opinion about language and its functions and purposes, the chances are that the usual response to the question, 'What is language used for?', would be 'for communication'. The typical respondent to the question might well want to add 'Of course!', thereby suggesting that an obvious question only invites an obvious answer. It is indeed a commonplace to suggest that language is for communication. Frequently, in universities and colleges of advanced education, language studies are taught within departments and schools of 'communication studies'. In addition, the English language curriculum guideline materials issued by the various state departments of education tend to stress the importance of developing in children such things as 'the ability to communicate effectively', where this is seen very much as a language matter. It is at best a superficial judgment, however, to suggest that language is mainly for communication, for such a judgment touches not at all upon the particularly powerful role of language in the ordering of experience. It is with language that we create that which is to be communicated: information is born of experience, but, equally, experience for normal members of the community is largely shaped and articulated by language.

Language is a resource with which human beings structure and organise their experience. So constantly is language in use in the complex behavioural patterns in which people engage in the course of conducting their daily affairs that its true significance is frequently ignored. A model of language primarily as an instrument of communication implies the having of some information, attitudes(s), ideas(s) or point(s) of view to be conveyed to others. By constrast, a model of language as a resource implies the having of a tool with which to **construct** information, attitudes, ideas or points of view. Furthermore, a model of language as primarily a mode of communication carries the additional implication that persons first hold some information, attitudes, ideas or points of view and then, as it were, 'give' or 'pass' them on to others. On the other hand, a model of language as a resource for the construction of information or ideas carries the implication that many persons participate in the processes of construction: that ideas or information are not simply held and passed on to others, but are actually shaped in the patterns of interaction in which people engage.

Language serves so many purposes that it is rarely that we can claim that any passage of language satisfies only one purpose. Whether people are using language to tell a story, give a lecture, make love, order a meal in a restaurant, seek directions about how to reach some destination, or discuss the probable consequences of a nuclear war, they seek both to influence and/or relate to others in some way, and to negotiate some kind of information, understanding or feeling. That is to say, language is used partly to initiate, maintain and foster relationships, and partly for the negotiation of a 'content' of some kind. Broadly speaking, both kinds of purposes are a feature of the language used in most situations. Both profoundly influence the nature and patterns of language.

Language in the classroom

Consider Texts 1 and 2, which are from familiar classroom situations in two Year 1 classes. In both, a range of behavioural patterns and of associated meanings are negotiated by teacher and students. Try reading the texts out loud the better to get some sense of the human interests and needs being served in each case. As you read, bear in mind and stop from time to time to answer the following questions about both texts:

1. How do you know these texts are from school situations?
2. Who is responsible for structuring the situation in each case?
3. How are the participants—teachers and students—negotiating meanings?
4. What kinds of expectations about who will talk and what will be talked about appear to apply?
5. What kind of language capacities and prior experience do the children appear to need in order to participate successfully in each situation?

Text 1   A Show and Tell session in Year 1

1	Mrs L.:	Okay . . . everybody ready now for Show and Tell.
		[Mrs L. looks around the group sitting in front of her on the floor. She sees Cathy with a book about the Melbourne Zoo.]
2		OH, you've got a lovely book there, Cathy. Is that the zoo
3		one? [Cathy nods her head] . . . that one that Howard brought
4		along before? I don't think we had much from that . . . You
5		can start, please.
		[Cathy stands up from the group of children on the floor in front of Mrs L. and moves to the front where she takes the teacher's place, Mrs L. moving off to one side.]
6	Cathy:	Good morning, girls and boys.
7	Chorus:	Good morning, Cathy.
		[Cathy shyly displays her book, opening it at a page of coloured photographs of animals.]

2

Child:	Can you show us the tigers?	8
	[Several others make remarks *sotto voce*, e.g. 'I've been to the zoo'; 'I like the monkeys best'; 'We saw some cockatoos'; 'I know how much they are'—the last a reference to the price of the book.]	
Cathy:	[Turns to a page but what she says is so indistinct it is impossible to hear.]	
Mrs L.:	Hold it up so that everyone can see.	9
	[Mrs L. starts to read a large notice printed in the book.] 'Please do not feed, or tease or attempt to disturb . . .' Who can read the last line?	10 11
Joel:	'Animals'.	12
Several children:	'Any of the animals'.	13
Mrs L.:	Yes . . . 'any of the animals'! Why don't you go around feeding all the animals with your ice cream and your Twisties and your lollies and your peanuts? Veronica?	14 15 16
Stephen:	Makes 'em sick.	17
Veronica:	Because they don't like it.	18
Mrs L.:	[ignoring Stephen] Yes, and also?	19
Michael:	They might die.	20
Mrs L.:	Yes, they might die, and also?	21
	[Pause—the children appear unable to respond because of uncertainty over what Mrs L. is referring to.]	
Mrs L.:	When do animals get fed first? Remember the book I read to you yesterday?	22 23
Child:	In the morning.	24
Mrs L.:	Yes, in the morning, and very often they don't need to have too much food, they'll get too fat and unhealthy. So if you keep feeding them more, they will get sick.	25 26 27
	[Cathy points to a picture of tigers.]	
Cathy:	There was one walking up and down. Dad tried to take a photo. There was three all asleep . . . Two woked up and stared at us.	28 29 30
Child:	Which was your favourite?	31
	[Cathy points to a leopard.]	
Mrs L.:	The leopard . . . mmm.	32
	[Cathy points to a peacock.]	
Cathy:	That one was walking around out of its cage . . . People were throwing rocks at it.	33 34
Mrs L.:	Oh, that's not a nice thing to do, is it? What is it, Deborah?	35
Deborah:	[reading from the page] 'Peacock'.	36

3

37	Mrs L.:	There's a bird there called a kingfisher. The other name is
38		a kookaburra . . .
		[Inaudible]
		[Cathy turns to a picture of an aviary.]
39	Geoffrey:	Spider web [a reference to the appearance of the aviary].
40	Mrs L.:	What is the spider web for then, Geoff? Do you know?
		[Geoffrey remains silent, uncertain of the answer.]
41	Child:	Birds.
42	Mrs L.:	What's the spider web made of, Stephen? Do you know?
43	Stephen:	Steel and iron.
44	Mrs L.:	Steel and iron. But they'd fly through the gaps, wouldn't they?
45		What's between the gaps in the iron and steel, Joel?
46	Joel:	Wire?
47	Mrs L.:	Is it wire or is it glass?
	Children	
48	together:	Glass.
49	Mrs L.:	Cathy, you were there. What do you think it is in the gaps
50		between the frames?
51	Cathy:	It looks like glass.
52	Mrs L.:	It looks like glass. You think it's glass, too, Wendy, do you?
53	Wendy:	Plastic glass.
54	Mrs L.:	Or is it plastic glass? I haven't been there for a long time, so
55		I don't know. Gabriel, would you put your pad back on your
56		table, please? [A reference to the item Gabriel has brought
		to show and tell about. Mrs L. is signalling that Gabriel is
57		inattentive.]
58		You'll get your turn maybe later on. But not now.
		[Gabriel moves back to his desk from where the class group
		is seated on the floor and places the pad on it. He then returns
		to sit with the other children.]
59	Child:	[reading from the book] 'A rainbow parrot'.
60	Mrs L.:	A rainbow parakeet or a rainbow 'lorikeet'?
	Several	
61	children:	Lorikeet.
62	Mrs L.:	Steve, sit down. You're bumping people and Aaron's got a
63		very sensitive nose at the moment. [Aaron has earlier told
		Mrs L. that he has had a 'blood nose' and has been told by
		his mother not to blow it.]
64	Mrs L.:	I think there's a little bower bird down there, Cathy. Bower
65		birds make a little bower or a little kind of cage thing to go
66		into. Down the bottom [she indicates on the page].
67	Cathy:	We saw the seals.
68	Mrs L.:	Did you? Did you like them?

Joel:	What did they eat?	69
Mrs L.:	What did they eat, Cathy?	70
Cathy:	Fish.	71
Child:	Where did they eat the fish?	72
Cathy:	They went under water and just went 'golp' [making a swallowing action and noise].	73
Mrs L.:	[pointing] What is that animal?	74
Deborah:	It starts with 'p'.	75
Mrs L.:	It's a 'black-tailed prairie dog'.	76
Geoffrey:	Mrs L. . . . I know how bats hang.	77
	[Mrs. L. ignores Geoffrey.]	
	[Cathy points to a picture of a cockatoo.]	
Mrs L.:	Isn't he pretty?	78
Cathy:	We saw the cockies in the cage. There was different colours of them. Birds and things would come into this cage . . . [indecipherable] . . . None of them would say hello.	79 80 81
Mrs L.:	Well, that's very good, Cathy. I think it's time for someone else. Will you choose a boy, please?	82 83
Cathy:	Aaron.	84
	[Cathy vacates the chair and sits on the floor while Aaron moves to the front to take her place.]	

Text 2 The early morning period in Year 1

Mrs B.:	Good morning, everybody.	1
Children:	Good morning, Mrs B.	2
Mrs B.:	Say good morning to Miss Christie.	3
Children:	Good morning, Miss Christie.	4
Miss C.:	Good morning, girls and boys. Ooh! I've got a frog in my throat today! [clears throat] Good morning, girls and boys. That's better.	5 6 7
Mrs B.:	Move back a bit, Jodie.	8
	[Indecipherable . . . directing children to move about a bit. Children are moving about where they sit but essentially they are ready for the day. Mrs B. begins to mark the roll.]	
Mrs B.:	Now . . . [indecipherable] . . . Christopher?	9
Christopher:	Yeah.	10
Mrs B.:	Robert?	11
Robert:	Yeah.	12
Mrs B.:	David?	13
David:	Yeah.	14
Mrs B.:	Frankie? Still away. Karl?	15 16

17	Karl:	Yes.
18	Mrs B.:	Tony? Away again.
19	Mrs B.:	Mark?
20	Mark:	Mmm.
21	Mrs B.:	Michael?
22	Michael:	Yes.
23	Mrs B.:	Simon?
24		Michael P_____ here? No.
25		Three boys away. All right one, two, three, four, six . . . must
26		be getting rid of a bad cold. David, keep that still for a bit
27		please [a reference to his toy in a plastic shopping bag].
28		Emma?
29	Emma:	Yes.
30	Mrs B.:	Luelle?
31	Luelle:	Yes.
32	Mrs B.:	Kerrie?
33	Kerrie:	Yes.
34	Mrs B.:	Stacey?
35	Stacey:	Yes.
36	Mrs B.:	Daniela?
37	Daniela:	Yes.
38	Mrs B.:	Meaghan?
39	Meaghan:	Yes.
40	Mrs B.:	Kate?
41	Kate:	Yes.
42	Mrs B.:	Carrie?
43	Carrie:	Yes.
44	Mrs B.:	Tracey Mc_____?
45	Tracey:	Yes.
46	Mrs B.:	Danielle?
47	Danielle:	Yes.
48	Mrs B.:	Narelle?
49	Narelle:	Yes.
50	Mrs B.:	Emily?
51	Emily:	Yes.
52	Mrs B.:	Vanessa?
53	Vanessa:	Yes, Mrs B.
54	Mrs B.:	Tracey?
55	Tracey:	Yes, Mrs B.
56	Mrs B.:	Belinda?
57	Belinda:	Yes, Mrs B.

Mrs B.:	Elizabeth?	58
Elizabeth:	Yes, Mrs B.	59
Mrs B.:	and Jodie?	60
Jodie:	Yes, Mrs B.	61
Mrs B.:	. . . [indecipherable] . . . Um, Danielle . . . [gestures towards her desk with the roll she is marking] So . . . somewhere on my desk. Put it under the container that's got the pencils in it [a reference to the roll she has been marking and has finished. Danielle is being asked to put it away].	62 63 64 65
Mrs B.:	Let's sing our morning song.	66
Children & Mrs B. together:	Good morning, good morning, And how do you do? Good morning, good morning, And a happy day to you. Good morning to you, Good morning to you. We're all in our places, With bright shiny faces, And this is the way, To start our new day.	67 68 69 70 71 72 73 74 75 76
Mrs B.:	That's good. Lunch orders? Kelly, keep that still please [a reference to a bag being rustled]. David? [He nods.] Stacey?	77 78 79 80 81
Stacey:	Yes.	82
Mrs B.:	Have a think as your names are being called out whether you've got one popped in your bag and you haven't put it out. [The 'one' here refers to any lunch order the children may have brought from home but forgotten.] Luelle?	83 84 85
Luelle:	Mmm.	86
Mrs B.:	Kelly? . . . and um . . . Tracey—Tracey Mc._____? Right . . . one, two, three, five lunch orders . . . David, Stacey, Luelle, Kelly and Tracey. Anyone else? Right, Kate you can take that down to the canteen, please. [Kate leaves the room carrying the lunch order.] Newstime? News? Come out first, Christopher, please.	87 88 89 90 91 92

[Christopher comes out to stand next to Mrs B. and faces the other children who remain seated on the floor.]

93	Christopher:	Good morning, Mrs B. Good morning, girls and boys.
94	Mrs B. & children	Good morning, Christopher.
	Christopher:	[indecipherable—speaks very quietly]

[The object produced is a yellow plastic racing car with the number '50' on it. Mrs B. takes and holds it up.]

95
96 Mrs B.: [pointing to a winding up device] What's that make it go, does it?

[Someone volunteers to explain.]

97 Well, let Christopher tell, please.

[Christopher operates the motor and produces a whirring sound.]

98
99 Oh, that's really good, isn't it? What's that number on the front, Christopher?

100 Christopher: 5.

101 Mrs B.: Yes, but what's the whole number?

102 Christopher: Um.

103 Mrs B.: It's a big number.

104 Child: I know.

[A number of children start to call out.]

105 Several children: 50.

106 Mrs B.: Right, well, you tell us, Kelly [not one of the children who called out].

107 Kelly: 50.

108
109 Mrs B.: Right, number 50 in the race. What else have you got there? Where did you get them? [Christopher produces two or three smaller cars.]

110 Christopher: My dad.

111
112 Mrs B.: Your dad . . . well, how did you get them? I mean, did you buy them?

113 Christopher: No. I don't know where he gets them.

114
115 Mrs B.: [holds up smaller cars] Lots of lovely, lovely cars. Are there many Geelong ones? [A reference to the fact that one car is blue and white—the colours of the Geelong football team.]

116 Christopher: Mmm.

117 Mrs B.: Which is your favourite team?

118 Christopher: Um . . . [his manner suggests uncertainty about his team].

Mrs B.:	Who do you barrack for?	119

[Christopher appears confused and remains silent. The question produces a number of animated if fairly quiet responses from the other children, e.g. 'Geelong', 'Essendon', 'Hawthorn'.]

Right, well, you pop them all in and put them over on the shelf 120
[He puts them in a plastic bag and places them on the shelf as directed]. David? Did you bring your things? [David nods.] 121
Well, you can bring them out, please. 122

Comparing Texts 1 and 2

Texts 1 and 2 are drawn from very much longer passages of discourse. None the less, for the purposes of this discussion they will be referred to as Text 1 and Text 2. In Text 1, one activity, and in Text 2, five activities are negotiated and concluded.

In Text 1, Cathy is invited by her teacher, Mrs L., to be the first person to present some object or information as part of the daily Show and Tell session. She brings her book about the Melbourne Zoo to the front of the class, and a passage of discourse develops around the information provided in the book both in photographs and in written text. Cathy is rewarded by her teacher for her efforts and invited to nominate a boy to take a turn at Showing and Telling, on the pattern applying in her class by which boys and girls alternate. Cathy nominates Aaron and moves to sit down, making room for him to assume the Showing and Telling role. Henceforth, like the other members of her class, she must assume a different role: that of the audience for whom Aaron and subsequent other children, assisted by their teacher, will offer information.

Essentially, one activity has been negotiated: some aspects of the animals found in Melbourne Zoo have been briefly explored. The manner in which such aspects are selected and explored is determined by several factors: partly, of course, by Cathy's choice of book, the pictures she selects from it and the kinds of observations they prompt from the experiences of both Mrs L. and the other children. At a more profound level, the factors shaping the nature of the activity relate to the roles assumed by the various participants and to their relationships vis-à-vis one another, most notably in the expectations about each other's behaviour implicit in these roles and relationships.

In Text 2 there are five activities, each of which constitutes a different stage in the overall pattern of activity. In the first line the teacher, Mrs B., and the children in her Year 1 class exchange greetings with each other and with me (I was present on one of my regular weekly visits). During the process of greeting each other, the children are taking up their positions on the floor around Mrs B. who sits on a small chair at the front of the room.

In the second activity, Mrs B. marks the role. She nominates each of the children in turn, they acknowledge their nomination, and if a child is absent, the silence that ensues after his or her nomination is normally sufficient for Mrs B. to note the absence.

9

In the fourth activity, Mrs B. determines which children need to place lunch orders in the school canteen, and whether the children have the necessary money. Once this is resolved, a child is told to take the orders to the canteen.

In the fifth activity, Mrs B. invites Christopher to present some news in the Morning News session. Christopher stands up and moves to the front of the group, bids everyone 'Good morning', and the children solemnly bid him 'Good morning' in return. Christopher produces some toy cars and some discussion of these develops, guided by Mrs B. When Mrs B. judges Christopher to have been given sufficient time for discussion of his toys, he is asked to put them away. Another child is then nominated to present his Morning News.

The activity in Text 1 is very like the fifth activity in Text 2, though there are some differences, the nature of which we will consider more fully a little later. While we may view the activities in Text 1 and Text 2, part (v) as very similar, it will be apparent that they are very different from the other activities in Text 2. In fact, each activity is markedly different: each involves the participants in undertaking different tasks and responsibilities. Because the tasks and responsibilities differ as much as they do, the behavioural demands made upon the participants in each case—most notably the demands on their language—differ in quite fundamental ways.

Chapter 2

Identifying the overall pattern, form or structure in Texts 1 and 2

In noting one major activity in Text 1 and five in Text 2, we have drawn attention to the presence of overall behavioural patterns negotiated by the participants in each case. The evidence for the presence of such patterns is linguistic evidence. In both cases, language is used to structure—and hence make sense of—some aspects of experience. The structure is of a familiar kind—familiar, that is, both to us, who have all been to school ourselves, and to the particular children involved, all of whom were in their second year of schooling when the two sessions were recorded, and had been participating daily in similar kinds of activities for a number of months.

Familiarity with what is going on does not in itself, of course, ensure equal proficiency among participants involved in a language-using situation. Not all the children involved were, in fact, able to participate with comparable skill, particularly in the kind of activity identified in Text 1 and in part (v) of Text 2. We may well pose a question here: When all children are participating in the same discourse in the classroom, why should some manage better than others to get a sense of how to proceed linguistically? Differing explanations are offered from time to time, some ascribing the cause to differences in intelligence, others to differences in social background. One thing is clear: what counts as school failure is a pupil's inability to recognise and use the language that is necessary for mastery of the various kinds of school learning.

Ability to manipulate the language necessary for school learning is a matter of **knowing how to do it:** how to go about constructing the various patterns of discourse in which different kinds of knowledge, information and ideas are expressed or **realised**. Even in very simple passages of discourse such as Texts 1 and 2, particular patterns do, in fact, apply. That is to say, certain methods of using language are employed here to shape experience in particular ways, and hence to create particular kinds of information and ideas. The overall pattern or structure that emerges may be thought of as a form or a GENRE, having a staged, orderly sequence of steps through which meanings are made.

A discussion of the ways in which genres are created, and of the factors responsible for them, is provided by Hasan in *Language, Context and Text: Aspects of Language in a Social-Semiotic Perspective*, by Halliday and Hasan (1989).

The term 'genre' as it is used here is an extremely important one, and it will be extensively used in other parts of the series. The term is important because in using it we intend to draw attention to the fact that language use is never random and never unstructured. Even in casual conversation, as will be suggested elsewhere, there is always a structure or an overall pattern or order in which language is used. If, indeed, students of this series have used the term 'genre' before, it will probably have been in the context of literary discussion: different works of literature are frequently described as 'genres' to differentiate one particular form, e.g. the sonnet, from another e.g. the lyric, the ode, the short story, or the novel. As the term 'genre' is used here and elsewhere in the series, it refers to any staged and culturally purposive activity leading to the creation of a text. We create texts representative of particular kinds of genres to serve different social purposes. A number of genres are representative of school practice, and all of them may be thought of as 'curriculum genres'. The Show and Tell or Morning News sessions are representative of two similar curriculum genres.

The genre of Text 1

Let us return to some of the questions posed before the reading of the texts and consider the nature of the curriculum genre in Text 1. How do the discourse patterns reveal aspects of the relationships of Mrs L. and the children? What kinds of meanings are being made and what are the contributions of the respective participants to those meanings?

Mrs L:
(1) initiates the activity (l.1);
(2) prompts Cathy in a manner intended to help her show and tell effectively (l.2);
(3) assumes a Showing and Telling role to provide a model for Cathy (l.10–11);
(4) asks questions of the other children to elicit responses relevant to the issues and/or ideas raised by Cathy's book (l.14–16, 40);
(5) responds to the children's responses to her questions (l.25)
(6) attempts to elicit remarks and/or observations from Cathy in her Showing and Telling role (l.40);
(7) praises Cathy (l.82); and
(8) concludes the activity (l.82–83).

Cathy:
(1) greets the other children (l.6);
(2) appears uncertain about how to proceed and which aspects of the book to turn to or talk about (between l.8 and 9);
(3) responds to the prompting from Mrs L. to hold the book up higher (between l.9 and 10);
(4) offers some observations about her recent visit to the zoo (l.28–30, 33–34);
(5) answers one question asked of her by Mrs L. (l.51); and
(6) nominates Aaron to succeed her (l.84).

The other children:

(1) greet Cathy (l.7);
(2) ask occasional questions of Cathy (l.8, 31);
(3) respond to Mrs L.'s questions (l.17−18, 20); and
(4) occasionally offer Mrs L. information which she ignores, mostly for its apparent irrelevance to the matter in hand (l.77), but also sometimes because she has an objection to a child who calls out without being asked to speak (l.17).

Overall, a pattern does emerge: a greeting establishes the relationships of the Shower and Teller and the audience; a series of observations and elicitations follows, in the course of which some items of information or ideas—some meanings—are jointly constructed; and the activity concludes. Of course, the pattern does vary from time to time and depending upon the particular child in the Showing and Telling role.

Children who are more comfortable with the role tend to behave differently from Cathy. For instance, Aaron, the child she nominates to succeed her, is very comfortable with the role of Shower and Teller. He always relaxes with ease into the designated chair and proceeds to address the class with confidence on whatever item of news or object interests him. He frequently tells jokes: sometimes, something his sister has said or done; sometimes, something he has seen on television which has amused him. He occasionally directs a question to the group and, when he sees someone who is apparently not paying attention, he is even capable of calling the person to order, assuming a disciplinary function as one aspect of his authority role as Shower and Teller! He always brings his session to a conclusion by saying 'finished' or 'I've finished', and, without prompting from Mrs L., he selects a girl to succeed him.

The pressure upon the person who assumes the Showing and Telling role, is in fact, quite considerable. Keen is the competition, for the most part, to be the person nominated to move to the front and talk, but, once there, children quite frequently founder, at a loss to proceed after the obligatory greetings have been exchanged. In fact, of the various elements of the Showing and Telling role, the only one with which all children seem comfortable is that of bidding the others 'good morning': knowing how to proceed after that, how to select and marshall items to talk about, how to conclude, and who to select as a subsequent Shower and Teller, are not matters all children find easy. Some, like Cathy, have considerable difficulty, and they need support and much practice in order to become more proficient.

Rarely, if ever, is the problem caused by a child's having nothing to talk about: Cathy, for instance, has a book and the memory of a very recent visit to the zoo to talk about. The problem, rather, is in knowing **how** to talk about the matter in hand: how to use her linguistic resources so as to reconstruct her experience of the zoo visit, thus enabling her to share aspects of her private experience. This requires something we expressionistically call 'organising' information; linguistically, this amounts to the selection of patterns that are relevant to the particular activity. The activity necessitates the taking of certain roles and hence the assumption of certain responsibilities. The role of Shower and Teller is that of an authority whose status is publicly acknowledged by being placed in a prominent position in front of the class (actually the teacher's position), and by being required to exchange formally polite greetings with the rest of the class. Of course, the ultimate authority who has decreed that the activity will proceed as it does is the teacher, Mrs L.: hence, as we have already noted, she prompts Cathy as she does to enable her to become more effective in her Showing and Telling role.

What is it that the Shower and Teller is really required to do in this situation? In fact, to answer this question accurately we need to examine many such texts before we can claim the presence of an established curriculum genre. However, the very considerable body of data from which Text 1 derives confirms that it is quite representative and that we can therefore generalise with some confidence from the particular example under discussion.

Primarily, the Shower and Teller's role, once the position of authority has been assumed and the greetings concluded, is to address the class either about an object, as in Cathy's case, or (as is frequently the case for Aaron) about an incident or an event. To do this, the Shower and Teller must make statements representative of some item(s) of his or her experience and must make them, furthermore, in such a way that they will excite some questions or statements from the audience. Together they must create a text in which all participants contribute, in their different roles, to the construction of shared meanings and understandings. Once the Shower and Teller has made what may be considered sufficient statements and/or excited some kind of appropriate responses, the activity is brought to a close.

The term 'transitivity process' comes from systemic linguistics, as discussed by Halliday (1985). It refers to the experiential process that finds expression in verb forms. A transitivity process reveals 'what's going on'. Six transitivity processes may be identified:

1. Action or material, e.g. He <u>ran</u> home.
2. Mental, e.g. I <u>believe</u> your account.
3. Relational, e.g. She <u>is</u> the Queen.
4. Behavioural, e.g. He <u>laughed</u> aloud.
5. Verbal, e.g. She <u>spoke</u> loudly.
6. Existential, e.g. There <u>is</u> somebody at the door.

Notice the kind of language Cathy uses in her Showing and Telling role, and how it contrasts with that of other participants in the text. To recreate and represent past experiences of her recent zoo visit, she uses the declarative mood throughout, and she moves into the past tense as in lines 28 and 33. The TRANSITIVITY PROCESSES of which Cathy talks, and which are identified in the verbs she uses, are for the most part to do with the actions of the animals and sometimes of the people visiting the zoo.

Some examples will illustrate the point. ACTION OR MATERIAL PROCESSES include the following: *there <u>was</u> one <u>walking</u> up and down* (l.28); *Dad <u>tried to take</u> a photo* (l.28–29); *that one <u>was walking</u> around out of its cage* (l.33); *people <u>were throwing</u> rocks at it* (l.33–34); *they <u>went</u> under water and just <u>went</u> 'golp'* (l.73); and *birds and things <u>would come</u> into this cage* (l.80). Several other processes are what are termed BEHAVIOURAL PROCESSES: *two <u>woked</u> up and <u>stared</u> at us* (l.29–30). Others are MENTAL PROCESSES, e.g. *we <u>saw</u> the seals* (l.67); and *we <u>saw</u> the cockies in the cage* (l.79). The final process Cathy uses is very close to an action or material process though technically it is classified as a VERBAL PROCESS: *none of them <u>would say</u> hello* (l.81). Processes to do with the state of being of the animals are very few in Cathy's discourse. Some, which are known technically as EXISTENTIAL PROCESSES, include: *there <u>was</u> one . . .* (l.28); *there <u>was</u> three . . .* (l.29); and *there <u>was</u> different colours of them* (l.79–80).

14

Note, by contrast with Cathy's discourse, the large number of inter-
rogatives in Mrs L.'s discourse (1.10−11, 22−33, 45). Note also the ways
in which she and the other children employ the present tense: it is always
for the realisation of different kinds of meanings from those using the
past tense. The transitivity processes found in Mrs L.'s discourse tend
also to include some which are material, e.g. *hold it up* (1.9); *why don't you
go around feeding all the animals?* (1.14−15); and *they'd fly through the
gaps* (1.43). Others are existential, e.g. *there's a bird there called a
kingfisher* (1.37). A RELATIONAL PROCESS is found in *what is the spider
web for then, Geoff?* (1.40). There is a mental process in *so that everyone
can see* (1.9), and a behavioural in *who can read the last line?* (1.10−11).

In fact, a number of the kinds of transitivity processes found in Mrs
L.'s discourse do not differ very much from the kinds in Cathy's
discourse. What does mark Cathy's passages as different from those
of Mrs L. is that in Cathy's case material processes predominate: she
mainly reconstructs elements of what happened and what she saw at
the zoo. Such experiences are realised mainly as actions. It is noteworthy
that Cathy uses no items to do with personal attitude or evaluation.

It should be noted that no one feature of Cathy's choice of linguistic
items is necessarily more important than any other in the construction
of her representation of experience. Indeed, in order to be successful
in using language at any time, she must draw upon quite a complex
interconnecting set of possible choices in the linguistic system. The
consistent use of the declarative mood and of the past tense, and the
very high incidence of material or action processes collectively contribute
to the building up of a recounting of aspects of her experiences. There
are, of course, many other linguistic items at work to which we have
not even drawn attention. We have identified enough for the moment
to suggest how the role Cathy assumes as Shower and Teller causes
her to exercise certain kinds of linguistic choices in order to create the
kinds of meanings appropriate to the activity in hand.

One interesting observation needs to be made about the roles of
the various participants in Text 1. To judge from the body of data from
which it derives, it is an observation which appears to hold true for all
such Show and Tell curriculum genres. The function of evaluation—of
passing judgment upon something said—remains that of the teacher alone.
Proficiency in this kind of genre actually requires that the Shower and
Teller produces reasonably sustained observations about events,
happenings and experiences that we may assume the children actually
did find pleasurable. None the less, the actual language they are
encouraged to use by the terms of the curriculum genre generated by
the teacher is on the whole non-evaluative—it is value free. In Text 1,
for example, in lines 35 and 82 it is Mrs L. who offers evaluative
comments, in both cases by the use of a relational process of attribution:
Oh, that's not a nice thing to do, is it?, and *. . . that's very good.*

Why, we may well ask, do children not use language for such a
purpose in this particular genre? The explanation must lie in an examination of the teacher's role: she is the authority figure who not only
largely determines the series of teaching−learning episodes over the day,
but is also the ultimate arbiter concerning what constitutes acceptable

15

and unacceptable behaviour, what will be deemed good or bad. An unacknowledged lesson learned by the children in their participation in genres such as that in Text 1 is respect for the teacher's authority.

As we noted earlier, language is so intimately part of the total behaviour patterns in which we engage and interact with others that its true significance is often overlooked: values and attitudes about power and authority, about good and bad manners, about what it is appropriate to refer to and what to remain silent about are all variously acknowledged and expressed in the ways in which we use language. All these matters are elements in the processes of children's learning in schools.

The demands made upon language for school learning are different from those applying outside school, though as yet we lack sufficient research evidence that can fully illuminate the differences. Children such as Cathy and Christopher are capable of producing texts involving both the reconstruction of experience and the expression of personal attitude and feeling. Indeed, they no doubt regularly do so, both in the school playground and at home. Suppose, for example, that Cathy were to tell her friends in the school playground of her visit to the zoo, and to show them her book. She would almost certainly produce a more complex text than that reported above, and that may seem somewhat surprising, since in one sense the two activities may seem alike. However, the two are not alike, for what is at issue in the classroom is mastery of a particular kind of curriculum genre that is part of the culture of schooling. The genre, as we have seen, operates in such a way that certain constraints apply, and it is these that determine the roles taken up by the participants, and hence the kinds of texts they are required to construct.

The genres of Text 2

It will not be necessary to deal with each of the genres in Text 2 in great detail. They have all been included principally to make the point already indicated above: that each activity does, in fact, impose different language demands upon the children, though they are not all equally important for success in school learning. Each requires that children learn how to use the language necessary to deal with each activity. The point may seem somewhat laboured. No great capacity is required, it may be suggested, to exchange morning greetings, to answer one's name in a roll-call, or even to sing a song! Well, that does depend upon the point of view—more specifically upon the prior experience—of the person(s) in question.

Berger and Luckman (1966) provide an interesting discussion of the social construction of meaning, and of the role of language in this process.

Behavioural patterns are learned: they are learned in the processes of participation in many different socially created situations. Central to the processes in which persons interact in situations, together shaping perceptions about what is going on, and about what value it has, is the use of language. Language is one of the most significant resources with which people make meanings. In order to participate successfully in the various situations in which they find themselves, particularly in schools, children need to learn the language necessary to deal with these situations. Anyone who has observed young children in the first months of schooling will remember how long it can take them to master the practices of morning greetings, roll marking, singing morning songs and so on. Anyone interested in the significance many young children attach to mastering these, and other rituals and routines of schooling, should observe them playing at being at school both in the year or two before they formally commence school, and often, once started, after school hours. Such play involves frequent practice in the patterns of behaviour—particularly the language—that are a feature of the routines concerned.

All school learning—for all age groups and across the different content areas—involves learning language: learning the ways of shaping information and ideas that characterise the different school subjects and/or learning activities.

To return to Text 2: Mrs B. has, in fact, had conversation (including some exchange of greetings) with most if not all of the children in the classroom before the nine o'clock school assembly in the playground, or at the assembly, or as they all moved back into the school room. Why, then, does she have them go through the activity of exchanging morning greetings again, with herself, and with the visitor? Why, furthermore, having worked her way through the roll, does she return to the theme of morning greetings with the song, and finally, why does she also expect Christopher and the other children to exchange morning greetings yet again?

If we were to ask Mrs B. herself her reasons, she would probably answer that she is interested in teaching good manners to the children; in addition, that the singing of the song after the opening roll-call breaks the pattern and allows everyone an opportunity to talk after a period during which only one at a time might speak; finally, that for the purposes of the fifth activity and genre, the exchange of greetings is a normal requirement whenever any child is selected for Morning News.

We should accept these explanations, noting only in addition at a more profound level certain other points. Firstly, the frequent exchange of greetings is part of the ways in which the various activities are demarcated the one from another, and hence given definition. Secondly, as we saw in Text 1, the authority of the teacher as the figure who decrees what will happen, and to whose requirements the children do in fact accede, is also being subtly acknowledged. It is difficult to imagine many other situations, after all, in which a group of people so frequently exchange morning greetings within the space of the twenty minutes actually involved! Thus, as we noted much earlier in this discussion, language serves both to mediate and maintain relationships, and to negotiate 'content' or information of some kind.

Looking specifically at the fifth genre, it is apparent, as we have already noted, that the pattern is very similar to that of Text 1. The role of Newsgiver (Mrs B. prefers 'News Time' to 'Show and Tell') is taken by Christopher. He is rather less successful in fulfilling the role than is Cathy. He greets the class and produces an object, a car, one of several he has brought in a plastic bag. His opening remark is inaudible.

Look closely at the five points at which Mrs B. attempts to elicit a response from Christopher. In ll.95–96 the attempt to draw Christopher into explaining how the car works, though well intentioned, simply causes him to demonstrate its working by actually operating the mechanism. It is, in fact, a very reasonable response to the question, *What's that make it go, does it?*, though the primary object of the whole activity is to cause Christopher to talk.

The second question, in ll.98–99, invites a one-word answer, and even that Christopher is unable to provide. The third question, in ll.109, invites a short response: *My dad.* Note that to this point the questions—all in the present tense—have sought to elicit short factual responses from Christopher. There is, of course, nothing wrong necessarily with such questions: they may even, in some cases, be a necessary prelude to questions which invite rather more from children. The fourth question (ll.111–112) is interesting, however, because it provides evidence of the kinds of language abilities best suited to this situation, and of the teacher's probably unconscious attempt to develop these abilities.

The fourth question marks a shift in direction and purpose, as Mrs B. plainly intends to direct Christopher towards constructing an account of how the cars were obtained by his father. To do this, she moves to the past tense, inviting Christopher to recall and reconstruct what happened. Why does Mrs B try to direct Christopher in this way? It is because in this situation, for the purposes of this kind of genre, the most productive way to use language is actually to recreate some episodes, events or happenings in the child's life. In fact, as the person who spent many hours in the classrooms observing and also recording the discourse involved, I can affirm from the data amassed that those children who are successful in the role of Shower and Teller or News-giver are those who do construct accounts of something done with family or friends, something bought in the supermarket, something seen on the television, something said at dinner time, some occasion celebrated, and so on. It will be recalled that Cathy, diffident and shy though she was, was most successful when she recounted some incident at the zoo. Children more skilled even than Cathy at the activity, and at the ways of using language relevant to the genre, need considerably less assistance in selecting appropriate linguistic items with which to construct meanings relevant to the Showing and Telling or Newsgiving role. That is to say, they know **how to mean** for the purposes of this activity.

It was Halliday (1975) who first suggested that learning the mother tongue involves learning how to mean. Painter (1989) discusses the early language development of her child in *Learning the Mother Tongue*.

In the event, in Christopher's case, though the question designed to elicit an account fails to do so, it none the less does cause Christopher to produce his longest utterance. The fifth question, in ll.117 and 119, in which Mrs B. returns to an attempt to elicit a simple factual answer, produces no more from Christopher, and the activity is brought to a close.

Proficiency in learning situations can be demonstrated to be heavily dependent upon developing the language abilities necessary to deal with those situations. The more teachers can become aware of the kinds of language abilities needed in different learning situations, the more they will themselves be enabled to direct and guide their children's learning. This is a theme to which we will return later.

One difference between Text 2 and Text 1 is worth commenting on: the other children in the group ask no questions of Christopher but some do of Cathy. Judging by the evidence of the many recordings made in both classrooms, that is because Mrs B. tends unconsciously to operate in such a way that the other children have less capacity to initiate and elicit information than they do in Mrs L.'s class. She asks most of the significant questions, because she sees this as part of her role in assisting the Newsgiver. More than she realises, however, the effects are firstly, to cause the Newsgiver to direct his or her newsgiving statements particularly towards herself; and secondly, to leave the other children fewer opportunities to elicit statements from the Newsgiver than are available to the children in Mrs. L.'s class.

Despite the differences, enough has been said to demonstrate that essentially the same kind of genre applies in both Text 1 and in Text 2, part (v). The Newsgiver offers a morning greeting to the group, a series of statements and questions follows, the discourse is brought to a close, and another child is nominated to give news. As in Text 1, the function of offering evaluative comment remains with the teacher [see ll.98 and 114 in Text 2, part (v)], and, as we earlier noted, this fact subtly underlines the nature of her role as authority figure. There are other ways in which both the nature of the teacher's role as authority figure and her view of what constitutes good manners are reinforced. Note, for example, the manner in which Mrs B. pointedly nominates Kelly (ll.106) to identify the number on the car: she is chosen because she has not called out, unlike a number of the other children.

The construction of meaning in a genre

This book began with the claim that language is a resource for the construction of information, attitudes, ideas or points of view and went on to suggest that such a model of language is an infinitely more powerful one than the conventional view of language as an instrument of communication.

In what sense, then, may we say that, in the two texts we have discussed, language is used to **construct** meanings? Focusing particularly on all of Text 1 and part (v) of Text 2, it has been already established that a particular genre—a particular staged pattern of discourse—applies in both. In inviting the children to participate each morning in the construction of such genres, both teachers can have no idea what items of news and/or objects the children may choose to bring to present to the class. The individual Shower and Teller or Newsgiver—particularly a skilled one, like Aaron—may well know what he wants to focus upon or stress in presenting his information. But even he, once the opening statement has been made, can have no prior knowledge of the questions and/or statements his opening may provoke from either the teacher or the children. In other words, the actual items of information constructed—the meanings made—are determined by the joint participation of children and teacher. It is not the case that the meanings are simply conveyed by the Newsgiver to the others. The point holds regardless of the relative magnitude of the contributions of different participants.

What it is about which meanings are made is quite unpredictable: it is a function of the individuals concerned, their differing experiences, personalities, tastes and interests. **How** the meanings are made is, on the other hand, predictable. A behavioural pattern applies, and it must apply, if the participants in the teaching–learning activity are to operate together with any degree of sense at all.

In a teaching–learning activity there will be a complex set of behavioural patterns, not all of them language patterns. The movement to the front of the group, the taking of the teacher's chair, the production of a book or a toy car: all are essential elements in the teaching–learning activities we have been considering. In school situations in particular, however, language patterns and the capacity to recognise and manipulate them are essential elements in learning.

In learning how to mean in any situation, one learns how to construct the discourse appropriate to that situation: one learns, in fact, how to construct and comprehend different kinds of generic patterns in texts and how to make sense of them. The point holds as much for the young children whose texts we have been examining as it does for older students. At all stages of schooling, the meanings to be negotiated and understood in the various content areas or school subjects find expression in characteristic patterns of discourse, both spoken and written. It is these that children must master in order to be regarded as successful in their school learning.

A discussion of language and its role in school learning is provided by Lemke (1989) in *Using Language in the Classroom*.

Is the Show and Tell genre a 'good' one?

In arguing that learning language is learning how to mean, it has so far been suggested that what is involved in such a process is a matter of learning to recognise and manipulate the various patterns of discourse characteristic of different situations and/or activities. The young children involved in Texts 1 and 2 are learning to participate in an activity in which the primary responsibility of the Shower and Teller or the Newsgiver is to make fairly sustained observations about some object, activity or event. The authority of the role and the status it is accorded have been already noted.

What are we to say of the teacher's objects in involving the children in participating in such activities and in producing such genres? The practice of instituting Show and Tell sessions or Morning News sessions applies in many Australian infants and junior primary school classes, and its usual justification is that it fosters oral language development. Like most such claims, the latter has some truth: certainly a number of children in the classes of which Christopher and Cathy were members did appear to develop fluency and confidence in the Showing and Telling or Newsgiving role, and the children seemed to enjoy these sessions.

The claims for the educational value of Show and Tell and Morning News sessoons are at best rather questionable, however, for several reasons. In the first place, the commitment to promoting oral language as something independent of other areas of language development is itself very dubious. The notion of language development must involve development both in speech and in literacy, and no very useful distinction can be drawn between the two. They are necessarily very closely related.

Furthermore, even the children who are successful in Showing and Telling or Newsgiving will benefit from being given opportunities to use spoken language in other ways in schools. The particular activity and genre are not uniquely suitable for the development of oral language abilities.

On the contrary, since the particular genre used at any time is itself dependent upon the activity concerned, it should be clear that the need is to generate a range of differing activities in schools, to enable children to master the associated range of genre types. Regrettably, Morning News and Show and Tell sessions frequently feature as the only concessions made to the development of oral language in daily school programs. Where this is the case, the language program is impoverished indeed. In a good language program children move easily through many learning activities of a kind designed to stimulate and extend abilities to speak, to read and to write. In justice to Mrs L. and Mrs B., I should perhaps note that neither teacher was committed to the view that the Show and Tell genre was the only one through which to develop oral language.

Chapter 3

Language, ideology, culture and schooling

At one or two points in the discussion to this point, reference has been made to the ways in which values and attitudes are variously realised in patterns of language. We referred, for example, to the ways in which the authority and status accorded the Shower and Teller are acknowledged. We referred also to the authority of the teacher, and we noted that values concerning what constitute good and bad manners are apparent in both Texts 1 and 2. All these values about authority, status and appropriate behaviour, and many others of a like kind typically expressed in school situations, are aspects of the ideology of schooling in Australia. Ideologies may be thought of as sets of beliefs, attitudes, myths, assumptions and values associated with social groups, institutions and classes. Society at large has ideologies of many kinds, and the differing groups within society have ideologies as well.

The difficulty for us in dealing with ideologies lies in understanding how unconscious yet pervasive and powerful they are. We have no trouble, for example, in acknowledging that the Australian Constitution and the Australian legal code involve important ideologies and sets of beliefs about how we will live, and about what actions will be condoned and what not condoned. However, the ideologies that operate are often unexpressed and therefore powerful levels are frequently harder to acknowledge.

Issues to do with language, ideology and culture are dealt with by all contributors to the series. In particular, Kress (1989) considers such matters in *Linguistic Processes in Sociocultural Practice*.

There are ideologies at work in schools, apart from those concerning persons and their relationships. These include ideologies concerning the nature of knowledge and the kinds of learning experiences children should undergo as part of their education. Such ideologies find expression in many ways, not all, of course, in language. They are expressed, for example, in the design of school buildings and in the design of the school grounds available to children to play in.

For example, some schools still have rows of desks bolted to the floor and arranged in such a way that all the children look towards the teacher and are really denied easy interaction with their peers. Others use open-plan classrooms where furniture is variously displayed and different working spaces are employed by students at different times of the day. Both patterns imply fundamentally different ideologies about human beings and how they learn, and about the purpose of schooling.

Some schools have extensive playing fields and grassed and treed areas, and perhaps adventure playgrounds. Others have relatively confined and sometimes concreted areas, which invite comparison with the exercise yards associated with prisons. Both offer important contrasts in their ideologies about childhood, about growing up, and about the kinds of physical movement and activity deemed appropriate for children.

At other levels, ideologies are expressed in organisational decisions about the pattern of the school day, most notably in the timetable. Some timetables lock children into a rigid day, while others are more flexible. At other levels still, ideologies are expressed in school programs and school textbooks, and in the various other curriculum materials found in schools.

At yet other levels, ideologies are constantly being shaped in the discourse of teachers among themselves, of teachers and pupils, and of teachers and parents. Outside the school, in the wider community, ideologies are also held about the nature of schooling, about the responsibilities of teachers, about children and the nature of childhood, about gender, about what boys will learn, about what girls will learn, about what is appropriate masculine and feminine behaviour—and so on. We could go on for a very long time without exhausting all the kinds of ideologies that operate.

The issue of gender is considered by Poynton (1989) in Language and Gender: Making the Difference.

The point to be noted about the presence of such complex interlocking kinds of ideologies is that they all impinge upon and have consequences for any particular teaching–learning activity we choose to isolate for examination. No teaching–learning activity is free of the impact of values and beliefs. In all teaching–learning activities, then, ideologies have important but often quite unacknowledged consequences for the kinds of expectations held of teachers and learners.

When children fail in school, I would suggest, it is frequently because they function with different understandings and perceptions from those of their teachers, and thus they use language differently. We learn language in order to mean. How we mean is very much a matter of experience and opportunity: a matter of the kinds of discourse we have learned to handle and of the associated values and behaviours we have learned to control.

The point has particular significance, for example, when we consider the education of Aboriginal children in Australia. Such children do not, on the whole, perform well in schools. Compared with many white children, they often begin school seriously disadvantaged in their efforts to learn and tend subsequently to become irregular in their attendance, finally dropping away altogether. Even when Aboriginal children continue to attend school conscientiously, they frequently fail to make the progress their teachers would really want for them. As an increasing number of researchers and educationists have begun to point out, the reason why such children perform badly is that they function with very different expectations from those of their teachers, and they do not really understand what is involved in learning in the ways their white teachers appear to value. The differences are, of course, of a sociocultural kind: differences in ideologies and beliefs, not only about what constitutes

These matters are discussed by Christie (1985) in the coursebook, Aboriginal Perspectives on Experience and Learning: The Role of Language in Aboriginal Education.

appropriate interpersonal behaviour, for example, but also about what kinds of knowledge might be worth acquiring, and, indeed, about how such forms of knowledge might be best acquired. All these differences find expression in the patterns of behaviour—particularly the language patterns—of Aboriginals and of whites. Even in the case of English-speaking Aboriginal children, a close analysis of the particular kinds of Aboriginal English dialects they speak reveals that such dialects operate to do different things from the dialects of white speakers of English. It is not the case that Aboriginal English dialects are inferior to those of whites: such dialects serve a range of important functions for the people who use them. Rather, it is that such dialects do not so successfully serve functions relevant to school learning.

Recent studies in America appear to support the same general conclusions about the significance of sociocultural experience and its expression, particularly in language patterns. For example, Brice Heath (1983) has reported on a major ethnographic study in which she examined three communities in the Appalachians. Two, a few miles apart, were communities of poor people working in the textile mills—one a predominantly white community, the other black. The third was the community of townspeople, black and white, in the neighbouring town. The effort to account for the greater success at school of the townsfolks' children over those of both poorer communities caused Brice Heath to conclude that differing behavioural patterns, including language patterns, were established from the earliest years of life, and that it was these that largely determined the varying responses of the children to the demands of schooling.

In a sense, the awareness has been around for a long time that different ethnic and social groups operate with differing though frequently unacknowledged experiences, perceptions and expectations, and that these find particular expression in language patterns. The work of Vygotsky (1934) and of Luria (1977), for example, was important in this connection. Bernstein (1973) argued that different social classes operate with different 'codes' of meaning, and that such an observation has very important consequences for the ways in which children of different social groups operate in schools. Specialists in the teaching of English as a second language to the children of the many families who have migrated to Australia have drawn attention to the manner in which differing perceptions of experience, attitudes, values and expectations are realised in the ways such children use language.

Not all specialists in the teaching of English as a second language share Bernstein's views, by the way.

Despite the fact that there has been an awareness of such matters, their full import, especially for education, has by no means always been acknowledged or understood. The work of Vygotsky and of Luria, for example, has found very fitful expression in the programs of schools of education in Australia, and Bernstein has often been dismissed, both in his own country, and in the USA and Australia. Those with specialist interests in the teaching of Aboriginals or of the various migrant groups in Australia have often in the immediate past felt that their claims and expressions of concern for their students were falling upon deaf ears.

No doubt a number of factors have been responsible for such a state of affairs. Partly, what was lacking was sufficiently rigorous

24

research evidence to support the claims that were made. Happily, that is changing: we now have more sophisticated research procedures—both linguistic and ethnographic—with which to support such claims, and the evidence can only continue to grow.

In addition, the proposition that persons are as they are, very much because of participation in the sociocultural contexts in which they live and develop, is for many a disturbing one. It challenges a centuries-old tendency in the Western cultural tradition by which a distinction is drawn between the individual and society, between the inner being and the outer world, between cognition conceived of as within the head and social interaction conceived of as of the outer world, where little relationship is understood between the two. It is part of a fundamental tendency to create dichotomies. Such dichotomies certainly have had some heuristic value: that is to say, they have served to assist investigation and enquiry into many matters, including the complex elements of human behaviour. But to acknowledge that such dichotomies have a heuristic value is not to claim, for the purposes of real practice, that the distinctions created by them actually exist.

These issues are discussed by Butt (1989) in *Talking and Thinking: The Patterns of Behaviour*.

For example, significant bodies of psychological research in the twentieth century have sought to study processes of learning, and to explore, in particular, elements of cognitive growth in children. There is a sense in which all educators are interested in how children learn, and such research has been not without its value. In practice, however, much psychological research has been based on a fundamental belief in the possibility of isolating either 'learning processes' or 'stages in cognitive growth', as processes and stages which will be shown to hold true for all individuals, regardless of sociocultural context. Such a belief in itself implies that persons have individuality—an inner being—for reasons other than social reasons. Their individuality, their cognitive and affective capacities, are matters that are innate.

It must be true, of course, that all persons are born with certain innate characteristics—characteristics that mark them as human animals, rather than other kinds of animals, and as different from other humans. If this were not true we would not all differ even physically, for example, as much as we do. However, whatever innate features children are born with, these features are made known to the rest of the world only through social processes: through the complex sets of interactions with others, which begin quite literally at birth and last as long as life itself. Whatever is innate is essentially what individuals bring with them into the world. But the world in which persons learn to develop and express their individuality is a social one, and, as we have suggested earlier, social situations differ from each other in fundamental, if often unacknowledged, ways.

We may well find evidence that particular kinds of learning processes appear to be representative of children in some group, but we should not therefore suggest that we have any evidence that such processes are typical of children in other groups. On the contrary, where such claims have been made, mostly unwittingly, many children can be shown to have been disadvantaged. To return to the example of Australian Aboriginal children for the moment, they have been shown to

The work of Harris (1980) is important here.

25

learn in different ways from those of many white children. No doubt many different groups of Aboriginal children in various parts of Australia differ from each other also. No one would suggest there is one way in which either Aboriginal or white children learn. None the less, in order to explain what has been the persistent failure of Aboriginal children to do well in schools, we must turn to the evidence that suggests that their behavioural patterns, including their characteristic language patterns, function to realise different kinds of meanings from those of the white teachers with whom, by and large, they have contact in the schools they attend.

We have suggested that one reason for the tendency to seek evidence for the presence of some innate, and hence presumably universal, learning processes and/or cognitive stages in persons has been that it is part of a centuries-old tradition to see dichotomies and to create distinctions that can be harmful. We have suggested further that the challenge to such a tradition is disturbing to some people.

We should note in addition two other expressions of concern frequently raised in discussions of the present kind. The first is an anxiety about the individual: the nurturing and fostering of the individual is one of the most prized objects of Western education. One has only to look at the various state curriculum guideline documents throughout Australia, covering all age groups and all school subjects, to note their universal commitment to the view that a prime object of education, regardless of who or what is being taught, is to develop individuals. Ideally, the educational system aims to produce happy individuals, capable of exercising judgment, independent in points of view, and confident in the expression of such views.

It is sometimes suggested that a preoccupation with the social context, and with the social settings in which persons develop and grow, implies a loss of concern for individuality: that arguments of the kind being advanced here might suggest that the significance of the individual is diminished, and that any society that tolerates such a thing is at risk. However, it is a confusion to suggest that a concern for the social context implies a loss of concern for the individual. On the contrary: a concern for a sense of the social context, as we are arguing it here, comes about precisely **because of** an interest in individuals and individuality. How shall we develop individuals? I would suggest here that persons achieve individuality through active participation in social processes, by learning to engage more and more fully in the various ways of meaning characteristic of their cultural context. This involves developing abilities of many kinds, including abilities to recognise and construct differing kinds of genres in listening, speaking, reading and writing. It is out of manipulation of one's own culturally created ways of making meaning that one learns both to express one's own individuality, and, ultimately, to develop new ways of making meaning.

The other expression of concern in this kind of discussion relates to the differences said to exist, on the one hand, between different racial and ethnic groups, and, on the other hand, between social groups and classes within any one group. The argument advanced here certainly espouses the view that there are differences: that, for example, Aboriginals are different from whites; that Vietnamese refugees who have recently arrived in Australia are different from the other ethnic groups with whom they mix in cities like Melbourne or Sydney; that within more or less homogeneous white communities, such as are still found in some parts of Australia, there are differences relating to social class. As we have already noted, it is being claimed here that these differences account in large measure for the varying school performances of children from these different groups.

But, it is sometimes said, if we take such a position, are we not actually finding a furtive way of reviving some very old and very unpleasant value judgments about the alleged superiority of some races and groups over others? Are we not, in somewhat more sophisticated terms than in the past, suggesting that different racial and/or social groups have different 'minds', and are we not admitting the possibility that some are better than others? There is a risk that the position argued in this series will be so misrepresented. Let us be very clear about what is involved here.

No scientist of any repute, as far as I am aware, has established the superiority of any race over any other, and there is no reason to believe such evidence will be forthcoming. Furthermore, were anyone disposed to look for such evidence, it would need to be of a kind different from that dealt with throughout this series, and certainly beyond the areas of expertise of its various writers. It would be evidence drawn from the work of those biologists, physiologists and neurophysiologists who investigate the actual composition of the human brain and how it works.

The argument being advanced in this series is based upon evidence drawn from careful and close observation of social patterns of behaviour. It is not drawn uniquely from the work of linguists or sociolinguists, but also from that of social anthropologists, ethnographers, phenomenologists, sociologists, social psychologists and educationists of many kinds.

In one sense, the argument advanced in this series **is** about a theory of mind. Once we have suggested that different social and ethnic groups operate in different ways, construct different kinds of meaning, and learn in different ways, we have advanced a theory of mind. But the theory is not, in the first place, about the superiority or inferiority of any one group compared with any other: it is a theory about difference. In the second place, it is a theory about mind as something socially created, and it advances no opinions about the physiological structure of the brain wherein the mind is located.

Certain inborn features of the brain must influence the kind of personality that develops as well as one's capacities to reason or to learn, and they must account in some measure for the individual differences we observe among people. But, as we have already noted, those characteristics that are present in an innate sense are known, made manifest, only out of participation in social situations. That is, the potential that persons are born with can be realised only in mastering various socially created ways of behaving, or ways of meaning. Whatever is inborn is so mediated by social processes that it is not possible usefully to think of the two as being separate and/or independent. The sociocultural contexts in which people are born and grow, then, profoundly influence the ways they operate, including, for example, the ways they relate to others, the ways they define and answer questions, and the ways they perceive and solve problems.

Even the processes we typically think of as mental—the private inner thoughts and feelings we all experience—are significantly influenced by the kinds of sociocultural contexts in which we operate: we internalise many aspects of our life experiences, and they thus become part of our inner life, influencing henceforth both the inner world of the imagination and the mind, and the outer world of activities and events in which we continue to engage. In this sense, the distinction between the inner being and the outer world in which we express our being is not clearcut, but very fluid.

This section began by suggesting that in significant ways ideologies are constantly being shaped and negotiated in many complex patterns of human behaviour, including patterns of using language. Ideologies, it was suggested, can be of many kinds. In school situations there are ideologies both to do with the nature of relationships and to do with the nature of knowledge: with what shall be learned and with how it should be learned. These ideologies, and the behavioural patterns in which they are expressed, are part of culture—part of the collective and complex sets of practices, beliefs, attitudes and values that mark a particular community of people as being alike, and hence different from other communities.

Cathy and Christopher, for example, and all the other children in their classes, were engaged in learning a number of aspects of the ideology of their culture. Some children were more successful than others, even at something as apparently commonplace and easy as Showing and Telling. Differences in school performance are frequently accounted for by suggesting that some children are 'slower' than others, that some 'apply themselves' more than others, that some are 'more attentive' than others. As **descriptions** of how children appear to present themselves in school situations, such judgments may well have truth: they have little, if any, explanatory power, however, and hence do not help teachers make appropriate decisions about how to improve the learning programs of their children.

The difficulty is compounded by the fact that teachers are often unaware of how different their own expectations may be from those of the children they teach. It has been hard enough, we are told, to encourage many white teachers to perceive that the learning difficulties of many Aboriginal children are difficulties born of a mismatch of culturally created values, attitudes and styles of working. It is often harder to encourage teachers to perceive that the difficulties of white children, say, in an inner-city Australian school are born of a like mismatch. It was this sort of issue to which Bernstein (1973) sought to draw attention when he talked of the ways in which children of different social groups operated with differing 'codes of meaning'. At the time he first wrote of these matters, as we have already noted, the evidence to support him, particularly the necessary linguistic evidence, was not really available. Now, as the whole of this series seeks to demonstrate, the research evidence is increasingly becoming available.

Language and learning: a sociolinguistic theory of learning

It has been suggested already that the position being argued in this book, and variously supported by the other authors in the series, really does involve a theory of mind. In the view adopted here, what we customarily think of as the mind, and the related notions of identity and of personality, are to be understood as socially created and sustained. It has also been suggested that conventional views of cognition, and the associated and very familiar interest in identifying 'stages of learning' common to all children, are of very questionable value. In fact, I am arguing here for the adoption of a view or theory of learning that departs in significant ways from many orthodox and familiar theories of learning as they have found expression both in university departments of education and in schools. It might be described perhaps as a 'sociolinguistic theory of learning', though, as I have noted elsewhere, the theorists whose work has variously contributed to this series include specialists other than linguists. What unites all such specialists is their commitment to the study of social processes and of the symbolic systems with which human beings negotiate and construct their understandings of experience.

In the sociolinguistic theory advanced here, language is to be thought of both as a resource with which we construct meaning and as a symbolic system with which we make sense of the world. We do, of course, use many other symbolic systems to make sense of the world and to build order into our lives: music, dance, painting and photography are some very obvious examples. All such symbolic systems are of great importance, but language has a particular claim on our attention as teachers and as educationists because of its significance in learning.

In an important sense, all learning in schools involves learning language. The point applies whether we are thinking about such areas of learning as those typically labelled 'primary language arts' and 'secondary English', or about such areas as mathematics. In the case of the former, it is commonplace to acknowledge that language has a role, but in the case of the latter, the significance of language is often overlooked. It is true, of course, that mathematics involves the manipulation of various mathematical symbols, but the processes by which these are manipulated, and the significance attaching to such manipulations, are none the less actually constructed in language. Linguistic processes are fundamental to all learning processes. Regardless of the content they teach, or the age group of their students, all teachers should see themselves as teachers of language, seeking to develop their students' language abilities.

Language development begins shortly after birth and it goes on as long as life itself, for, with the frequent entry into new situations and experience that is a feature of living, new language abilities constantly need to be developed. Language development may be said to have three interrelated elements: learning language, learning through language, and learning about language.

The first of these—learning language—refers to 'the building up of basic language resources: mastering the language skills of speaking, listening, reading and writing'.

The second—learning through language—refers to 'the capacity of using language to learn, articulate and express information abut one's world'.

The third—learning about language—refers to 'taking language as something in itself capable of examination—an object worthy of study. It can be studied as: (1) a **system** in terms of its meaning, grammar, vocabulary, phonology and writing system; (2) an **institution**, in its relation to the community, as a part of culture; or, (3) in terms of its **varieties**, by examining register or dialect variation' (Curriculum Development Centre, 1979, p.8).

M.A.K. Halliday was a consultant to the *Language Development Project*. The tripartite model of language development is one he suggested.

These three elements of language development are of course so interrelated that in many practical instances it is difficult to separate them. Certainly, from the point of view of the learner, learning language will also always involve some learning through language. Learning about language is not a necessary feature of all school learning, though it certainly does have an important place in formal education.

Of the three aspects of language development, it is learning through language that is the most enduring and pervasive. As we learn through language, we learn to construct a sense of relationships, experience, information and ideas. So enduring and pervasive is the power of language in the processes of the social construction of experience referred to elsewhere in this book that its significance is persistently overlooked and misunderstood. It is fundamentally important that we teachers and educationists do understand its significance: it is central to the sociolinguistic theory of learning with which we are involved, and whose implications we need to pursue in our teaching practices.

Language is learned in use, in the processes of dealing with issues of significance and importance to the learner. A moment's reflection on the processes by which young children learn language in their pre-school years makes this clear: learning the mother tongue is effortful, but the pay-off in terms of the child's developing capacity to do more things, to gain more things, to know more things, and to relate more fully to people is quite apparent to any parent watching the child grow. The principle that langue is learned in use applies, however, as much for children at school and for adults, as it does for the small child. We learn language and we learn through it, less because we ever set out to learn it and more because we enter into all kinds of CONTEXTS OF SITUATION in life in which the very need to deal with those contexts requires that we develop the appropriate behavioural patterns. Such patterns include the relevant language patterns.

Malinowski (1923) created the term 'context of situation' as part of an argument he developed about meaning in language. Any language has meaning only because of the particular context of situation in which it is used.

Hence, to return for a moment to the examples of Cathy and Christopher in Texts 1 and 2, in order for those two children to perform successfully in the context of situation that was the Show and Tell or Morning News session, they needed to develop appropriate language abilities. They needed, in particular, to be able to participate in the shared construction of one kind of curriculum genre: the Show and Tell or Morning News genre. Their particular role in that construction involved the production of statements or observations representative of some aspect of their own experience. As they struggled to produce the necessary texts through which to make such statements or observations, they were required both to learn language and to learn through it. That is to say, they had to select (not consciously, of course) the linguistic items appropriate to the construction of the text, and in doing so they learned to deal with one aspect of their own experience.

These general principles may be said to apply when we use language at any time. Some important educational principles would appear to follow. Firstly, if language is learned in use, as a consequence of engagement in activity and out of the need to deal with significant experience or information, then any educational practices that require students to be no more than passive recipients of information are by definition bad ones. Yet many Australian classrooms do operate in ways in which the primary responsibility upon students is to be just that.

Secondly, teachers need to focus upon the **behavioural patterns** their students need to master in order to become proficient in their learning. Once they start to do this, they will be enabled to make important changes in their curriculum practices. When planning their teaching—learning episodes, whatever the age group and whatever the subject area, teachers need to consider two questions:

1. *What do my students need to be able to do in language in order to be successful in mastering this content?*
2. *What kind of context of situation for working and learning should be generated in order that the students will be assisted to master the required language patterns?*

It will be in implementing their answers to these questions that teachers will put the sociolinguistic theory of learning into practice.

Chapter 4

Writing and schooling

To this point, the discussion of language learning has been based upon considerations of spoken language. There are good reasons for such a basis, since spoken language is both more enduring and pervasive than written language, and at the same time even more 'invisible' than written language. It is now appropriate to turn to considering written language, however, and in doing so we will pursue a little more fully some other aspects of the sociolinguistic theory of learning.

While the discussion so far has ranged across many aspects of spoken language and its role in the social construction of experience, we actually examined in detail only two texts, and, though Text 2 involved several sections that were representative of different genres, most of our discussion focused upon that section which compared most closely with Text 1. We thus have examined only one spoken genre of schooling. It remains for research to uncover and describe many others.

In turning to written language, our interest will be in considering those written genres that school experience would appear to require that children learn. If it is true that many values, attitudes, beliefs, information and ideas are variously realised in spoken langue, it is equally true that they are realised in writing. Just as learning to talk is a matter of learning to construct genres in which different meanings are realised, so learning to write is a matter of learning to construct different written genres.

Language for the representation of experience

Consider the following texts, all written by young children either in the Preparatory (Infants) Year or in Year 1:

Text 3
We made iale [jelly] today.

Text 4
Popcorn is delicious yummy and crunchy.

Text 5
My frens [friends] have a Dog its neam [name] is Priscess [Princess].

Text 6
My cat likes to get pats and he likes to play.

These are very representative of the kinds of texts young children tend to write in the first years of schooling. Where do they come from? What kinds of meanings do the children appear to be dealing with? What would appear to be their relationship to the written genres of older children, and indeed of the adult society?

Firstly, let us note that each text constitutes a statement about some aspect of the child's experience. Texts 3, 5 and 6 are statements in which no particular attitude on the part of the author is expressed in any way: they are, in fact, neutral in their tenor. Martin and Rothery (1981) have called such texts OBSERVATION GENRES. Text 4 is a little different, for it does involve an expression of attitude. Martin and Rothery (1981) have termed such texts COMMENT GENRES. Neither an observation nor a comment genre, it should be noted, is in any sense a 'story', though teachers often suggest that young children do write 'stories'.

Texts 3 and 6 were written by classmates of Cathy and Christopher. Interestingly, among the 54 children involved, particularly over the first 18 months of their schooling, though they wrote a large number of observation genres, examples of the comment form tended to be much less common. What significance are we to attach to this finding? What does it tell us about the kinds of choices in language the children are learning to make in their early writing, and how can we explain those choices?

Think back for a moment to the kinds of genres involved in Texts 1 and 2, and to the significance of the roles and relationships of those engaged in the discourse. The teacher in each case, we noted, not only tended to ask a significant number of the questions, but also tended to be the person who offered evaluative comments of some kind. As it happened, the writing activities in the two classes normally took place shortly after the Morning News or Show and Tell sessions. Invited to write about an aspect of their personal experience, the children tended to write much as they talked. That is, they offered observations about personal experience, only occasionally offering a comment as well as, or instead of, an observation. Of course, it was not the case that the children **could not** make comments: clearly they could, and often did, in contexts other than the Show and Tell or Morning News sessions. Rather, it was the case that the children were **constrained** by the demands set up for them in their discourse with their teachers to create the kinds of written genres that they did.

The latter is an important observation to stress, for it takes us back to the issue of language as an aspect of behaviour. What children learn to do in language is very much a matter of the behavioural demands made upon them. In order to be successful in the Morning News and Show and Tell sessions, as we have already noted, children are required to offer statements or observations about their experience. That is to

Martin (1989) pursues some of these issues in *Factual Writing: Exploring and Challenging Social Reality.*

33

say, in taking up the role of eliciting such observations, and in offering comments, teachers constrain the children to use language in particular ways. The fact that they **do** so constrain the children is in itself an appropriate thing: children will perhaps rely very heavily upon their teachers to guide them into mastering the ways of meaning—including the ways of constructing texts—that are valued and approved in schools.

There may be some readers who are at this point raising a protest. You may, for example, wish to argue that the Show and Tell genre is a limited one, or you may object to the absence of an opportunity for children to express personal attitudes or points of view. But this is a **different** issue. The issue we are attempting to identify here is this: that successful participation in any context of situation will require the ability to recognise and use the relevant discourse patterns or generic structures. In the Morning News or Show and Tell sessions, the children in the sample learned the lesson that their teachers valued in them the production of observations about experience. Hence, they tended to write such observations, as well as to speak them.

It may be suggested that we can have no certainty that all children writing observation genres and/or comment genres write them after Morning News. That is true of course, though it need not fundamentally challenge the basic argument here. If we concentrate on the ways in which teachers (and indeed many adults generally) relate to young children in particular, we find that they often try to elicit statements from the children about what they have been doing, where they have been going, and so on. In doing so, I would suggest, adults are actually encouraging children to engage in the reconstruction of experience. We must conclude that the invention, in English-speaking cultures at least, of the Show and Tell or Morning News session is itself one example of the tendency to encourage children to organise and reconstruct experience.

Capacity to use language to represent experience is developmental in that children do not develop language initially for such a purpose, though they do develop it later on. We need, however, to be careful about how we view the nature of whatever it is we term 'developmental'. Frequently, discussion of development in educational contexts carries the implication that there are 'developmental stages' through which children will pass, and that these have a presence in some innate sense: that is, it is held that all children will experience such stages as a matter of some inborn cognitive predisposition. Yet on the evidence of the research work cited here and elsewhere in this series such a claim seems unlikely. Certainly, we do appear to be genetically programmed to learn language, unlike other animals. However, whether we **do** in fact learn language, **how** we learn it, the **kinds of purposes** for which we use it, and the **kinds of meanings** we encode in it are all very much a matter of opportunity and of sociocultural context.

To take the matter of opportunity first, it is worth noting that there are recorded cases in history of children who have grown up in isolation from normal social intercourse, and they have not mastered a master tongue. In a few recorded cases, the children were confined to darkened rooms, or in other ways grossly deprived, while none the less being given sufficient food to sustain life. When they were discovered, these children exhibited few of the normal characteristics of social beings. Other cases are of children who grew up in the wild, leading the lives of animals. There is the famous case of the 'wild child' who was found living in woods outside Paris in the late eighteenth century and whose case was documented by the scientist Itard (1802), who took him into his home. (A very successful film on the life of the child was made some years ago by the French director, Truffaut.) In another case, in the 1920s in India, a Christian minister came across some children who had been nurtured and reared in a wolf pack, and who had become, effectively, members of that pack, having assumed behavioural patterns very much more akin to those of the wolves than to those of human beings, as we conventionally think of them. In all such cases, the children were denied access to the kinds of interaction with other human beings that would appear to be essential if children are to learn so many of the behavioural patterns we think of as being typically human, including the patterns of using language.

To take the issue of sociocultural context and its relevance for learning language, as was argued in an earlier section people learn to do differing things with their language depending upon the demands of social class and/or ethnic group. The point holds, as was earlier suggested, when we consider differences between Aboriginal and white Australians, and it also applies when we consider children of similar ethnicity, but of differing social groups. For example, if all the children in a school community speak English, it does not follow that they encode the same kinds of meanings in the language they use, as Bernstein (1973) sought to argue, and as Tough (1973, 1977), working with a differing methodology, also sought to demonstrate.

Whatever language capacity develops in young children, as indeed in all people at any stage of their lives, is profoundly dependent upon their sociocultural contexts and what these tend to generate and require in language. To return to the issue with which this short discussion started—namely that of language for the representation of experience—all children develop a language for the representation and reconstruction of experience. Yet not all learn to use language for such a purpose with comparable ease or success—not at least, in the terms required for school learning—as the earlier examination of spoken genres has revealed. It would seem that we should explain the differences by recourse to the differing domestic and social contexts from which children come.

The capacity to use language to represent experience is particularly important for school learning. It requires that children (1) 'pull back', as it were, from the activity or event of which they talk or write; (2) select from it the item(s) worth representing; and (3) construct a text in which such an item or items are rendered intelligible to others. Such capacity, once established in the early years, will be repeatedly called upon and extended for the purpose of learning in all subsequent years of schooling. Capacity to use language for the representation of experience, and subsequently for exploration, reflection, inquiry and argument, is peculiarly relevant for the kinds of knowledge and intellec-

Differences between
spoken and written
language as two
different 'ways of
knowing' are explored
by Halliday (1989) in
*Spoken and Written
Language*.

tual skills we value in the Western tradition of education. While such knowledge and intellectual skills are certainly developed in spoken language genres, they also find particular expression in the many written language genres. It is for this reason that good teaching practice should always pay careful attention to the kinds of written language genres that children need to master if they are to achieve an appropriate control of the various forms of school knowledge.

Writing and school knowledge

In many contemporary schools the children are frequently invited either to 'write a story' or to 'write about anything they like': free choice in what children write is for many teachers an important, even a fundamental, requirement. It is noteworthy that the concern with such freedom is found most commonly amongst infants and primary teachers when they are focusing on their language arts programs, and amongst secondary teachers of English. It is not generally a concern either at the primary level when dealing with subjects other than language arts, or at the secondary level among specialists in subjects other than English. The concern is associated with a particular view of the individual and of individual creativity. Children should be allowed to develop their individuality and their creativity, particularly in writing, goes the argument, and while it is generally agreed that the teacher will have some role in responding to children's writing, there is a strong feeling that teacher intervention and direction should be kept to a minimum. What matters is that the children should have 'space' and encouragement to express themselves as they wish.

The argument is a troubled and a confusing one. It rests upon certain serious misconceptions about the individual and about the nature of language in general, and of writing in particular. For reasons that have now been argued at some length in this book, I would argue that to use language at any time is to operate with a particular discourse pattern or a generic structure. Hence, whatever the subject about which children choose to write, they will need to select a discourse pattern or a genre through which to write about it. What they are able to select is very much **a matter of what they have been enabled to learn**. It is this aspect of the matter that is frequently simply not acknowledged, and children are left floundering. Teaching children about how written texts should be constructed should not be seen as imposing restrictions upon children. Rather, it should be seen as equipping children with a knowledge of the language patterns they need to grasp, and through which they will express themselves, and become original and creative.

Writing in subjects other than English

It is worth reflecting for a moment on why the particular attitude towards writing that we have identified finds very little expression among specialists in subjects other than English. If we were to ask teachers of social studies, of history, science, geography, economics, mathematics, and the like, what their priorities were in teaching their subjects, all would probably respond in terms that emphasised the acquisition by their students of some 'content' or knowledge. Some would also emphasise the development in their students of some mental skills.

On closer examination we will find that the mental skills valued in the different content areas are remarkably similar, as any review of curriculum guideline documents in the different subject areas in all Australian states will reveal. The skills include, for example, those of enquiry and investigation, of reasoning and of weighing up evidence, of researching and of assessing data. They also include methods and habits of judgment and discrimination, of persistence in undertaking inquiries, of exercising responsibility in dealing with information, of retaining an open mind while considering the relevant facts, and of being capable of working co-operatively with others in undertaking tasks. We might add to this list almost indefinitely, for a great deal has been written over the years in many official statements about the aims and purposes of education. All the skills and capacities that are identified, it will be clear, are valued as parts of the thing we term a 'Western education'. It is for this reason that they are valued across all the different subject areas, including the English language and literary studies.

If we turn from the mental skills to the content of the various school subjects, it is apparent that there are important differences. Specialists in the various areas of knowledge emphasise different phenomena for examination and enquiry, and their methods of dealing with the phenomena vary as well. In practice, particularly in the upper primary and in secondary years, when teachers plan and teach the various subjects they focus primarily on the content to be taught. Some never look beyond the content. Others, who do express an interest in the development of the mental skills referred to above, try to plan their teaching programs so that these skills will be developed in children while they are learning to handle the content. Rarely, in my observation at least, do teachers recognise the specialist language skills that the various subjects require.

In fact, it may be argued that learning any 'content area' or body of knowledge is primarily a matter of learning language: a matter, that is, of learning the particular discourse patterns within which are encoded the various ways of working that are characteristic of the different subjects. As was earlier suggested, there is a sense in which language may be thought of as 'invisible'. Certainly, as we use it, particularly in speech, we devote little if any conscious attention either to its grammatical patterns or to its discourse patterns. We tend to focus instead (for quite understandable reasons) upon the 'content' with which we are concerned, be that an activity, an event, or an idea. However, 'content' does not exist independently of the language patterns within which it is encoded, and through which, indeed, it comes into being. It is for this reason that teachers in particular must pay conscious attention to the various discourse patterns that their students need to learn in order to be successful in their school studies.

Of course, the development of the various mental skills alluded to as valued in Western education is also a language matter. Habits of inquiry, of considering and answering questions, of exercising judgment, and of researching and weighing evidence will themselves develop and find expression in the processes of dealing with significant bodies of information and ideas. To the extent that teachers will be enabled to judge the success with which such mental skills have been developed, they will make that judgment largely in speaking, reading and writing. The point is particularly relevant in the case of writing. Of the two productive modes of using language—speaking and writing—it is the latter that leads to a permanent and visible product on the basis of which teachers will perforce make considerable judgments about the success with which the students have learned. The enduring power of written examinations at all levels of education bears witness to the value attached to writing. And even in educational contexts that have abandoned examinations the students' capacities are still very heavily assessed on the basis of what they write.

We began this subsection by observing that teachers of primary language arts and secondary English attach particular importance to free choice for their students in determining what they will write. We suggested, furthermore, that such an interest in individual choice does not exercise the attention of non-English subject specialists to anything like the same extent as it does that of the English specialists. It does not follow that non-English specialists in general take much interest in language matters. On the contrary, most confine their attention to content and, to some extent, to the mental skills referred to above. These, as was suggested above, are typically thought of as independent of language patterns. To the extent that non-English specialists do address themselves to language issues, they tend, for example, to display lists of selected vocabulary items in the classroom, sometimes testing their students' ability to spell these. One would not wish to deny that learning different subject areas does involve learning relevant vocabulary or lexical items. However, it is misleading to imagine that learning the language of a school subject primarily involves learning words. Learning a subject at any level involves learning the ways of working, habits of inquiry, and methods of defining and answering questions characteristic of the subject in question. Such ways of working and patterns of inquiry really involve considerations both of the content to be dealt with and of the mental skills to be developed. To be proficient in a subject is, after all, not only to grasp a content, but also to understand how to use it. More specifically, however, we can say that both content and methods of working necessarily find expression—are indeed **realised** in—discourse patterns. Learning subjects is learning patterns of language wherein are trapped the various ways of dealing with issues and ideas characteristic of the different subject areas. Teachers of non-English subjects would do well, then, to recognise the role that language plays in their subjects, and specifically to build opportunities for their students to learn the generic patterns characteristic of their areas of work.

Writing in English language studies

To be fair, some teachers of primary language arts and of the subject English do have an interest in the nature of language, and they provide opportunity for their students to learn differing kinds of genres. However, somewhat paradoxically given the nature of their responsibilities, a very strong view prevails among many English teachers (at the secondary level, in particular) that their subject, unlike other subjects, is 'contentless': that its concerns are to do with the fostering of individuals through significant experiences, through the development of habits of reflection and perhaps of introspection, and through the development of capacities in self-expression. Since experience is by its nature multifarious, and since habits of reflection may be fostered in many ways, the argument goes, the 'content' of English defies definition. In the words of two recent authorities, J. Britton and J. Squire, it may be said of the content of English that

> it proves impossible to mark out an area less than the sum total of the planned and unplanned experiences through language by means of which a child gains control of himself and of his relations with the surrounding world.
>
> (Dixon, 1975, p. xviii)

The teachers of English who subscribe to such a view normally value in particular the significance and role of literature, and would want their students both to read literature and to create literary pieces of their own. It is for this reason that, in so far as any teaching and learning about the writing of English language genres takes place in English classes, it tends to focus primarily upon the writing of various forms of the narrative, and to a lesser extent, upon poetry. Few other literary genres appear to be dealt with. According to one recent Australian study, most other teaching and learning about language, in junior and secondary English classes at least, tends to perpetuate rather tired and sorry exercises in traditional grammar (Piper, 1983). Exercises in the pursuit of parts of speech, in the correction of grammatically inaccurate sentences, or in the accurate use of the various punctuation marks are a reasonably impoverished diet, if the concern is to produce confident and independent writers, able to select from a range of genres open to them and hence, also, able to generate new genres of their own.

Interestingly, a recent UK study of students' performances in writing at ages 11 and 15 has produced very similar findings (White, 1986).

That poor practices in teaching about the English language have survived for so long is symptomatic of a genuine concern of English teachers to undertake some language study with their students: in the absence of better models for the teaching of English, teachers fall back on some aspects of traditional school grammar teaching. Teacher education has been at fault for a very long time, in that it has failed to offer teachers more effective and rewarding models for teaching and learning about language.

Surely the content of English studies is the English language itself, in all its rich diversity. An imaginative focus by the teacher upon the ways in which literary genres are constructed should constitute a significant element of English studies. The imaginary or real-life experiences that are uniquely the concerns of literature will not be lost sight of if the English teacher has a genuine appreciation of the varieties of written English within which those experiences find expression. On the contrary, the sharper the teacher's perceptions of the distinctive linguistic features of the different genres, the better will be that teacher's capacity to guide and challenge students both in reading and in writing literature.

It will be recalled that, in our brief discussion of a sociolinguistic theory of learning, it was argued that language development involves learning language, learning through language and learning about language. Little was said about the last element. There is an important role for teaching and learning about language in many areas of schooling, though English studies will have a special contribution to make. English literature may be thought of as 'verbal art': language that is specially crafted in patterned ways that we value for the visions and perspectives upon human experience that it constantly offers. Part of the delight of literary study will lie in the exploration of how literature works.

Hasan (1989) discusses the term in *Linguistics, Language, and Verbal Art*.

But there are many other ways in which students will benefit from learning about language. The media—radio, television and film—all offer important areas for exploration. The varieties of spoken language found in the community are worth important investigation and inquiry: attitudes to differing speech patterns, and the kinds of judgments and even prejudices attaching to them, are all rewarding areas for students to examine. Finally, and most relevant to the present discussion, patterns of written expression merit study if children are to become proficient in their writing as they grow older. Processes of learning to write should begin as soon as children come to school, for, as my own research would confirm, the most successful early literacy programs are those that involve children in learning to read and write literally from their first week at school.

See Christie 'Some current issues in first language writing development' (1985) and 'Young children's writing development: The relationship of written genres to curriculum genres' (1985).

We will now consider some examples of written genres, with a view to demonstrating the point that even young learners must learn that different meanings are realised in different patterns of language.

Chapter 5

Some written genres by young writers

Early in Year 2, in common with her classmates, Cathy spent an enjoyable week in the period leading up to Easter. The children cooked Easter buns and made Easter eggs. Cathy wrote the following text about how to make chocolate Easter eggs. As you read it, consider these questions:

1. What kinds of choices did Cathy need to exercise in her selection of the linguistic items and the patterns in which they are used?
2. What kinds of meanings was she trying to make?
3. How would you describe the kind of genre Cathy has sought to create?
4. Do you consider it a successful piece of writing? If so, why is it successful?

Text 7   Chocolate eggs

Things we need
1. frypan [frying pan]
2. bowls
3. spoos [spoons]
4. mould
5. water

How to make them
1. ton [turn] on the frying pan low
2. pit [put] the water in frying pan
3. put chocolate in the bowl
4. melt chocolate
5. put the chocolate in the chaps [shapes] with a spoon
6. put them in the fridge
7. tack [take] them at [out] of the fridge
8. then poosh [push] them at [out] of the mould.

Most adults would have no difficulty in recognising Text 7 as a recipe. Martin (1985) identifies it as a PROCEDURAL GENRE. It is procedural because in it the child sets out to tell the reader how to do something.

Since I was present and indeed helped as the children made their eggs, and subsequently wrote about the activity, I can testify that the writing of such a text was quite effortful. It constituted a significant challenge for Cathy who was justifiably pleased with her effort once she had finished.

What kinds of linguistic features give this text its distinctive character, making it different from any other texts Cathy would typically read and attempt to write? When examining any text it is useful to begin by examining the transitivity processes about which the language is being used, and these are identified in verbs. It will be recalled that we made some examination of processes in the oral Texts 1 and 2. There are no processes identified under the first subheading, *Things we need*. There, Cathy simply names a number of items. But under the second subheading, *How to make them*, there are eight processes, and that information is itself significant in our attempt to understand the text. They are: *ton* (turn), *pit, put* [used four times], *melt, tack* (take) and *poosh* (push). These are all material or action processes.

Now notice the mood adopted with each process: in every case it is imperative. It is a text designed to direct action, and as such it is of a fundamentally different kind from a text, say, concerned with reflection upon action or event.

Several other features of the text are worthy of comment, for they all contribute to its status as a procedural genre. Its use of a heading and two subheadings is important: many other genres—stories, for example—never make use of subheadings. In addition, Cathy's use of numbers to identify the steps to be taken in undertaking the task of which she writes also serves to underscore its status as language designed to direct in a particular orderly sequence.

What did Cathy need to do in order to write such a text? As we noted earlier, she had to 'pull back' from that which she wrote about—in this case, the task of making Easter eggs—and she had to organise a sequence of steps for the reader to follow. To do this, she had to recall the steps herself and select the relevant linguistic items with which to construct the text. Procedural genres of this kind are very frequently found in English-speaking cultures: they are representative of some familiar and culturally important ways in which we go about dealing with experience. Recipe books, manuals and how-to-do-it kits are all familiar places in which such genres are used in the wider adult world. But such genres are also part of the language of school learning. For example, a great deal of the intellectual effort of much scientific experimentation requires that the student learn to organise and marshal experience in particular ordered ways, choosing the appropriate sequence in which various steps should be taken. Thus, as Cathy learns to write her procedural genre, she is also being inducted into one aspect of what is involved in marshalling information and in reasoning with it in a manner highly relevant to all her subsequent learning. She is learning language and she is also learning through language: for she is learning how to deal with experience.

Now let us look at Text 8, written by a classmate of Cathy, called Simone. As you read this text, consider the following questions:

1. What kinds of choices did Simone need to exercise in her selection of the linguistic items and the patterns in which they are found here?
2. What kinds of meanings was Simone making here? How did they differ from those in Text 7?
3. Do you consider this a successful text? If so, why is it successful?

Text 8   Zoo for sale

Onece [once] there was a zoo and there was a sign saying Zoo for Sale.   1
Some men were looking for a rhinoceros to buy. The next day all the animals   2
were awake and Wendy Mandy and I pinched the keys of the cages and   3
unlocked them and let the animals go free and take them to our school. We   4
tried to hide the animals they hid the camel like a hill and they hid the ostrich   5
like a light and the zebra like a gate and hid the other animals. It started   6
to rain and the animals came inside and the teacher rang the zoo keeper.   7
He came and took the animals and put them in their cages and took them   8
to Werribee Park. They liked Werribee Park better than the zoo and better   9
than our school.   10

[Note: the punctuation has been somewhat tidied up so to this extent Simone's text has been changed]

Most adults will have no difficulty in recognising this text as an example of a NARRATIVE GENRE, a kind commonly found in schools and frequently read to them in their first years of schooling. The text was inspired by reading another story with the same title. Simone was making extensive use of a narrative model available to her from her reading. In doing this, she was doing as we all must do: taking and adapting a generic structure that is common in our culture and creating her own meanings within that structure. As we get better, what we do in language is not normally so obviously derivative, but the processes of selecting from generic structures available and known in the wider culture will also apply.

If you have thought to examine the processes found in this text with a view to uncovering how it differs linguistically from Text 7 you will perhaps have noted the following: the opening processes, both of which are realised in *was*, are not action processes but existential processes: *there was a zoo* (l.1), and *there was a sign* (l.1). Most subsequent processes are to do with action: *were looking* (l.2), *pinched* (l.3), *unlocked* (l.4), *let . . . go* (l.4), *hid* (l.5), *came* (l.7), *took* (l.8), and *put* (l.8). A final process, to do with attitude, and hence called a mental process, is found in the last sentence: *they liked Werribee park* (l.9). Mental processes often appear at the ends of narratives, and they seem to constitute part of the way narratives are sometimes brought to a conclusion.

Most of the processes in Text 7, then, are material, a familiar feature of narratives, for they typically deal with the unfolding of real or imagined events over time. The presence of a large number of material processes is a characteristic Text 8 shares with Text 7, but for all that the two texts are not very similar. Wherein lies the difference?

The mood in Text 8 is very different from that of Text 7. Throughout Text 8 the mood is declarative, and, as will be immediately apparent, it is this that accounts for the extreme difference in the grammatical patterns of the sentences. There is another difference too: Text 8 makes use of linguistic items designed to tie the sequence of events together in a temporal sense. Thus, we find *once* (l.1) and *the next day* (l.2), though a sense of an implicit 'then' is apparent in several other places, e.g. *and* [then] *Wendy Mandy and I pinched . . .* (l.3), *and* [then] *let the animals go . . .* (l.4), and *it started to rain and* [then] *the animals came inside . . .* (l.6–7). Explicitly or implicitly narratives make extensive use of linguistic items that are to do with the sequence of events in time.

There are other matters we might take up about both Texts 7 and 8, but it is not necessary to do so here. We have said enough to demonstrate that procedural and narrative genres are fundamentally different, that their differences are differences in meaning, and that these differences are realised in different language patterns leading to the creation of differing kinds of texts.

Now let us turn to Text 9, our last written text. Michael wrote this text in the course of a unit of work on the children's suburb and its houses. The children had photographs of their houses, and after studying the real estate pages in the local paper, they wrote advertisements for their own houses.

Text 9   House for sale

[photograph]

This house is a big house at 2 Tolson Court. It in a quitt [quiet] court. It has a big garage. It has 3 bedrooms, a bathroom, with a bath and a vanity unit. It has a big lounge room.

$45 000

You are by now probably becoming familiar with what to look for in examining such texts with a view to teasing out the linguistic features that give them their character. The processes here, you will perhaps have noticed, are all relational: *is* (used twice) and *has* (used three times). Why is Michael constrained by the demands of the meanings he is making here to select these kinds of processes? The answer must be that it is because he is required to offer to the prospective buyer information in which he indicates what is the case. No actions are required, and expressions of attitudes, in so far as they find expression in processes, are not required here either. The mood is also declarative, though the text is not very similar to Text 8. That is partly because of the presence of the relational processes, but it is also because of the absence of linguistic items to do with temporal connectedness. No conjunctions are used either, and the item that more than any other ties this text together is *it*, which, after the first sentence, constantly refers back to the house.

In summary, then, Text 9 seeks to deal with very different experience from that of both Text 7 and Text 8. It does not direct the reader to action, as Text 7 does, nor does it seek to involve the reader in following a series of events narrated in sequence over time, as Text 8 does. It is a DESCRIPTIVE GENRE, whose purpose is to offer the reader detail about the subject described. It is a description of something in the 'real world', and not intended to be imaginative in any way.

Language as the 'hidden curriculum' of schooling

Texts 3—9 are representative of only a small range of written genres of the kind that children need to learn to handle as part of their schooling. Written genres, like spoken genres, as we have argued earlier, are expressions of different ways of making meaning. For all the learning experiences in which children engage throughout their years of schooling, they will be learning to make meanings in differing ways. As they do so, they will be mastering ways of working, ways of reasoning, ways of discussing, and ways of arguing, all of which find expression in the different subject areas of schooling. With progressive control of these ways of working, the children will increasingly learn to enter into the forms of knowledge and patterns of reasoning and of inquiry that are deeply part of the ideological traditions of Western culture.

It is the job of teachers to assist children to learn these matters. Where teachers are clear about the ways in which patterns of language work for the shaping of meanings, and for the development of attitudes and points of view, they will be themselves empowered. As teachers become empowered, so too they can empower their students, assisting them to enter with increasing confidence into the worlds of the imagination and of ideas, of inquiry and of speculation, and of argument and of debate. Unless teachers become conscious of the central role of language in the shaping of experience and of reality, and hence of its role in learning, language will remain invisible, and, as such, part of the 'hidden curriculum' of schooling. In justice, we owe it to all our students that we help to demystify the learning processes in which they engage, encouraging them to develop and control a wide range of ways of making meanings. In short, we owe it to them that we empower them, assisting them to move in increasing independence, and confidence, and hence in increasing control of their world.

References

Berger, P.L., & Luckman, T., *The Social Construction of Reality* (Penguin, Harmondsworth, 1966).

Bernstein, B. (ed.), *Class, Codes and Control*, vol. 2, *Applied Studies Towards a Sociology of Language* (Routledge & Kegan Paul, London, 1973).

Brice Heath, S., *Ways with Words: Language, Life and Work in Communities and Classrooms* (Cambridge University Press, Cambridge, 1983).

Butt, D., *Talking and Thinking: The Patterns of Behaviour* (Oxford University Press, Oxford, 1989).

Christie, F., 'Young children's writing development: The relationship of written genres to curriculum genres', Paper presented to the Language in Education Conference, Brisbane College of Advanced Education, Brisbane, 20–23 August, 1984, in B. Bartlett & J. Carr (eds.), *Language and Schooling: A Report of a Conference on Language in Education* (Brisbane College of Advanced Education, Brisbane, 1985).

Christie, F., 'Some current issues in first language writing development', Paper presented to the Annual Congress of the Applied Linguistics Association of Australia, Alice Springs, 29 August–2 September, 1984, in H. Nicholas (ed.), *Current Issues in First and Second Language Development* (Applied Linguistics Association of Australia, Melbourne, 1985).

Christie, M.J., *Aboriginal Perspectives on Experience and Learning: The Role of Language in Aboriginal Education*, ECS806 Sociocultural Aspects of Language and Education (Deakin University, Victoria, 1985).

Curriculum Development Centre, *Language Development Project: Phase II*, Occasional Paper no.1 (CDC, Canberra, 1979).

Dixon, J., *Growth through English: Set in the Perspective of the Seventies*, 3rd edn (Oxford University Press, Oxford, 1975).

Halliday, M.A.K., *Learning How to Mean: Explorations in the Development of Language* (Edward Arnold, London, 1975).

Halliday, M.A.K., *An Introduction to Functional Grammar* (Edward Arnold, London, 1985).

46

Halliday, M.A.K., *Spoken and Written Language* (Oxford University Press, Oxford, 1989).

Halliday, M.A.K., & Hasan, R., *Language, Context, and Text: Aspects of Language in a Social-Semiotic Perspective* (Oxford University Press, Oxford, 1989).

Harris, S., *Culture and Learning: Tradition and Education in Northwest Arnhem Land* (Professional Services Branch, Northern Territory Department of Education, Darwin, NT, 1980).

Hasan, R., *Linguistics, Language, and Verbal Art* (Oxford University Press, Oxford, 1989).

Itard, E.M., *An Historical Account of the Discovery and Education of a Savage Man, or of the Developments, Physical and Moral, of the Young Savage Caught in the Woods Near Aveyron, in the Year 1798* (Richard Phillips, London, 1802).

Lemke, J.L., *Using Language in the Classroom* (Oxford University Press, Oxford, 1989).

Luria, A.R., *Language and Cognition* (Winston, Washington, DC, 1977).

Kress, G., *Linguistic Processes in Sociocultural Practice* (Oxford University Press, Oxford, 1989).

Malson, L., *Wolf Children* (Western Printing Services, Bristol, 1972).

Malinowski, B., 'The problem of meaning in primitive languages', in G.K. Ogden & J.A. Richards (eds.), *The Meaning of Meaning: A Study of the Influences of Language upon Thought and of Science on Symbolism* (Routledge & Kegan Paul, London, 1923).

Martin, J.R., *Factual Writing: Exploring and Challenging Social Reality* (Oxford University Press, Oxford, 1989).

Martin J.R., & Rothery, J., *Writing Project Report, No.2, 1981*, Working Papers in Linguistics (Department of Linguistics, Sydney University, Sydney, 1981).

Painter, C., *Learning the Mother Tongue* (Oxford University Press, Oxford, 1989).

Piper, K., *Curriculum Style and English Language: The Investigation into Current Practices in the Teaching of English Language in Australian Schools*, ACER Research Monograph, no.19 (ACER, Hawthorn, Victoria, 1983).

Poynton, C., *Language and Gender: Making the Difference* (Oxford University Press, Oxford, 1989).

Senate Standing Committee on Education and the Arts, *A National Language Policy* (AGPS, Canberra, 1984).

Tough, J., *Focus on Meaning: Talking to Some Purpose with Young Children* (Allen & Unwin, London, 1973).

Tough, J., *The Development of Meaning* (Allen & Unwin, London, 1977).

Vygotsky, L.S., *Thought and Language*, Massachusetts Institute of Technology Press (Cambridge, Massachusetts, 1961).

White, J., 'The assessment of writing: Pupils aged 11 and 15', *Language Report for Teachers: 3* (Assessment of Performance Unit, Department of Education and Science, London, 1986).

Further reading

Berger, P.L., & Luckman, T., *The Social Construction of Reality* (Penguin, Harmondsworth, 1966).

Brice Heath S., *Ways with Words: Language, Life and Work in Communities and Classrooms* (Cambridge University Press, Cambridge, 1983).

Bernstein, B., & Henderson, D., 'Social class differences in the relevance of language to socialization', in B. Bernstein (ed.), *Class, Codes and Control*, vol. 2, *Applied Studies Towards a Sociology of Language* (Routledge & Kegan Paul, London, 1973).

Christie, F., 'Learning to write: A process of learning how to mean', *English in Australia*, no.66, December, 1983, pp.4–17.

Christie, F., 'Writing in schools: Generic structures as ways of meaning', in B. Couture (ed.), *Functional Approaches to Writing* (Frances Pinter, London, 1986).

Christie, F., 'Language and schooling', in S. Tchudi (ed.), *Language, Schooling and Society* (Boynton Cook, Upper Montclair, New Jersey, 1985).

Regan, J., 'Metaphors of information', in R.P. Fawcett, M.A.K. Halliday, S.M. Lamb & A. Makkai (eds.), *The Semiotics of Culture and Language*, Open Linguistics Series (Frances Pinter, London, 1984).

Technical terms

The meanings of these terms are either defined or implicitly given by the context where they first occur.